THE
CALIFORNIA
HOUSE

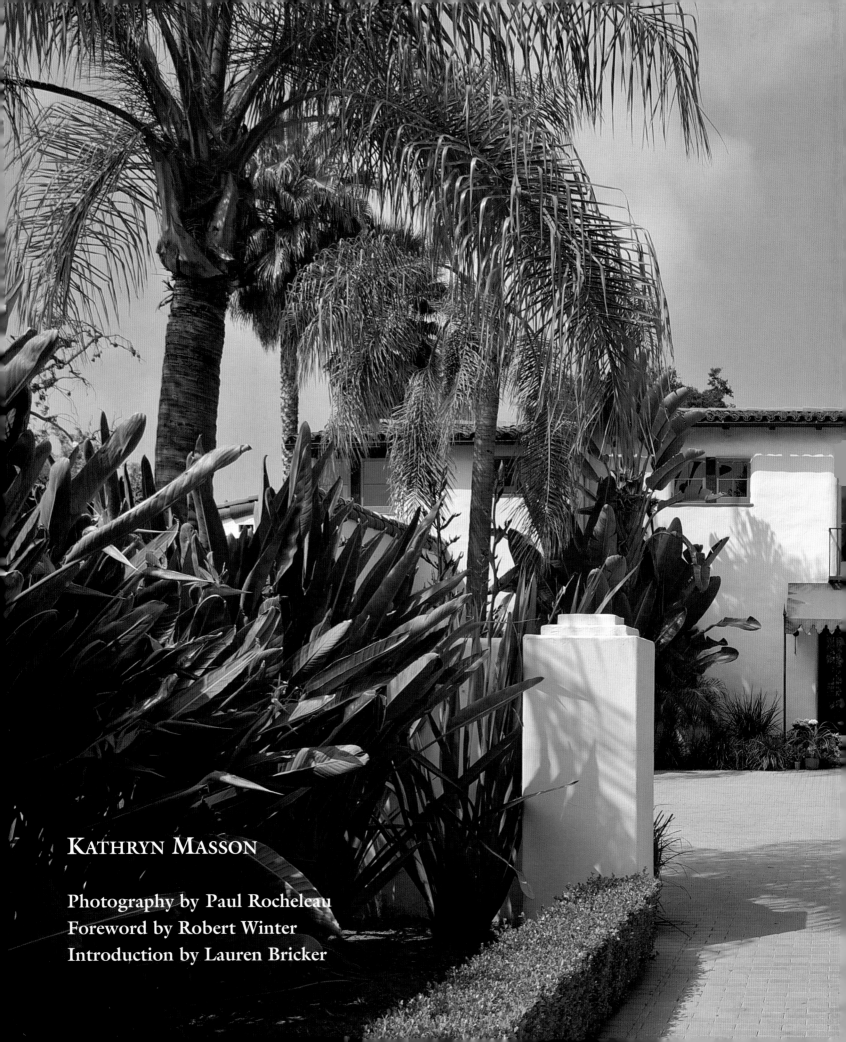

KATHRYN MASSON

Photography by Paul Rocheleau
Foreword by Robert Winter
Introduction by Lauren Bricker

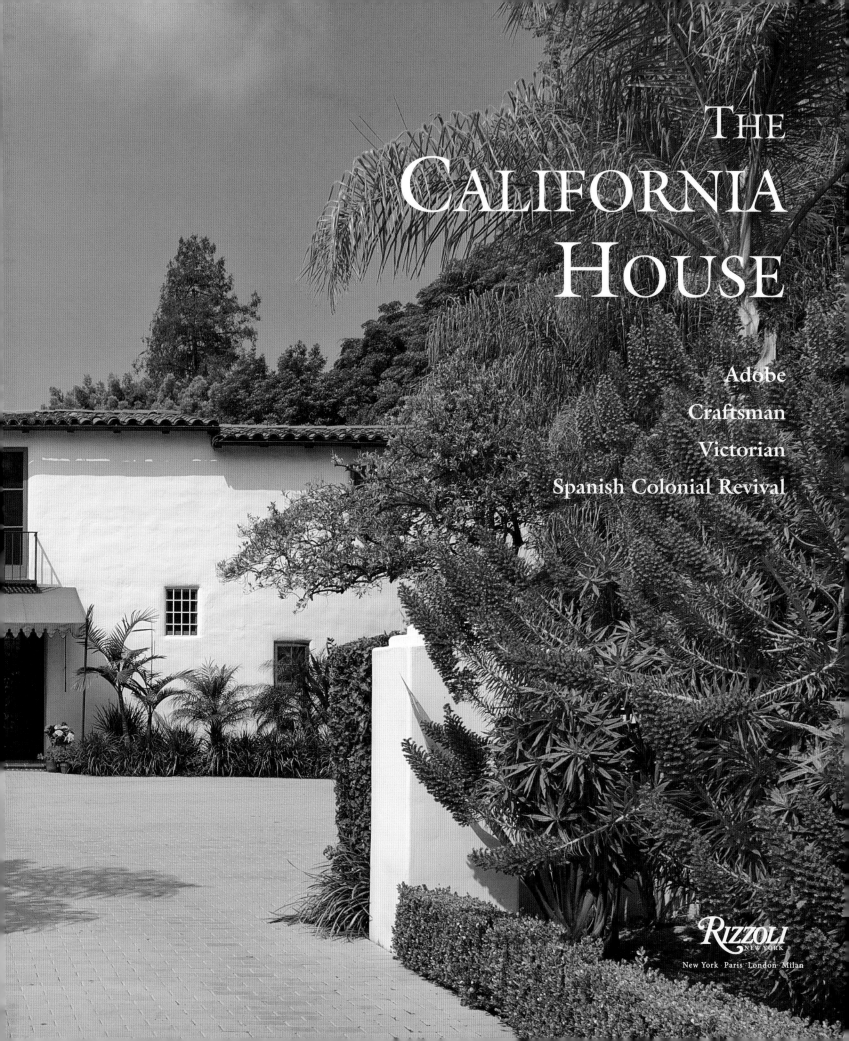

THE CALIFORNIA HOUSE

Adobe

Craftsman

Victorian

Spanish Colonial Revival

RIZZOLI
NEW YORK

New York · Paris · London · Milan

First published in the United States of America in 2011 by
RIZZOLI INTERNATIONAL PUBLICATIONS, INC.
300 Park Avenue South, New York, NY 10010
www.rizzoliusa.com

ISBN-13: 978-0-8478-3585-0
Library of Congress Control Number: 2010931531

Distributed to the U.S. Trade by Random House, New York

Page 1: *J. Henry Behrens House (Cuatro Vientos) (see page 222)*
Pages 2–3: *J. Henry Behrens House (Cuatro Vientos) (see page 222)*
Page 4: *William D. Edwards House (Casa Ru) (see page 186)*
Pages 6: *Fleishhacker Estate Gardens, Woodside (1927)*

Designed by *Abigail Sturges*

Printed and bound in China
2011 2012 2013 2014 2015 2016 / 10 9 8 7 6 5 4 3 2 1

This book is dedicated to

"El Jefe," Jarrell C. Jackman,

*executive director of the
Santa Barbara Trust for Historic Preservation,
who has kept the organization vital,
performed miraculous works of preservation
with his outstanding professional staff and
volunteers, and upheld the integrity of
Santa Barbara's Spanish and Mexican heritage
within the community for more than 20 years.*

Contents

Preface

Kathryn Masson

The California House was conceived as a brief historical journey through approximately a hundred years of California's early residential architecture from the 1830s through the 1920s. House choices represent an array of styles that begins with vernacular adobes and ends with a vernacular wooden farmhouse, including, in between, pattern-book-designed Victorians, architect-designed Craftsman bungalows, Arts & Crafts–inspired mansions, and period revival era houses, represented by the Spanish Revival and Spanish Colonial Revival styles. The book is not inclusive of all of California's diverse architectural styles, but it represents a visual continuum roughly from the vernacular adobe houses built by Spaniards and Californios (descendants of Spaniards living in California during the era of Mexican rule) to award-winning architectural masterpieces built in the Spanish Revival and Spanish Colonial Revival styles that sought to capture the feeling of Old Spain and early California.

Construction methods changed rapidly in California after the advent of the sawmill in the early 1840s. Labor-intensive adobe construction was replaced with that of wood frame. The linear plan and simplicity of the typical Mexican era house was replaced by elaborately decorated two- and three-story Victorian houses, whose ornate exteriors were often created from pattern-book designs cut with jigsaws. Although Queen Anne, Eastlake, and Italianate designs are found in virtually every region in America, San Francisco, with its vast multitude of ornate row houses and magnificent mansions, is the undisputed epicenter of magnificent Victorian architecture.

At the turn of the century the Aesthetic Movement in England spread to America and inspired houses that glorified the handiwork of man and the beauty of natural building materials as opposed to industrial advancement. Architects who are today honored as masters of this genre include Bernard Maybeck and the brothers Charles and Henry Greene. Also working within an Arts & Crafts aesthetic was young architect Irving J. Gill, who would become one of the most important architects of the twentieth century.

After World War I, Southern California became a mecca of prosperity and progress. Architects from the midwestern and eastern states arrived to find fledgling communities, such as Pasadena, Altadena, and San Marino, with welcoming opportunities for professional and financial advancement. These imports to California culture studied the architecture of Spain, Italy, and Mexico and familiarized themselves with the earliest adobes still existing in California. They then designed residences and commercial buildings that reflected this understanding. In residential designs that took advantage of California's mild climate, the designers also sought to capture the romance and beauty of a mythical past. Lush Mediterranean landscapes featuring water elements such as fountains and low-pitched roofs on wide verandas sought to capture a more relaxed lifestyle, reminiscent of Mexico and Italy. Men such as Myron Hunt, Reginald D. Johnson, Roland E. Coate, and George Washington Smith became well-published, award-winning practitioners of the Spanish Revival and Spanish Colonial Revival styles. Their work changed the built landscape of Southern California forever.

Foreword

R O B E R T   W I N T E R

My career in architectural history began in 1965, when David Gebhard and I began canvassing California looking for subjects for our architectural guides to the state. Over the years I have developed two massive and admittedly arguable generalizations: first, the most and best remaining architecture from the period before 1900 is in Northern California; and second, the most and best remaining architecture from the period after 1900 is in Southern California.

Northern California is full of small towns that have barely kept up with material progress. Old buildings tend to survive and be used in such environments. Even San Francisco, now a center of commerce, has retained the Victorian residential district called Haight-Ashbury.

Until 1900, Southern California developed more slowly. It had few small towns and those that existed have, with a few exceptions, been swallowed up by rampant developments that began in the twentieth century. Los Angeles itself, while smaller than San Francisco pre-1900, began to grow until today the city and county are virtually identical. Few reminders of the nineteenth century exist, but, unlike San Francisco, which went heavily for "urban renewal" in the 1960s, a number of early-twentieth-century buildings remain in the central city of Los Angeles.

Historians like reality. But what you see in modern restoration is often not what was originally there. It is usually an attempt to re-create history mixed with a wish to make the place look good to modern eyes. Adobes that once had tamped earth floors get new ones made of hardwood. Craftsman bungalows are furnished with Stickley or Stickley-esque tables and chairs that the original owner could not have possibly afforded. I should know. I live in such a bungalow. I have quite a few Craftsman pieces, but these are mixed with family heirlooms and things that I simply enjoy. Visitors often ask me, "What is original?" and I have to answer, "Nothing except the built-ins." The nicest reaction is when they say, "Well, it looks like home!"

This book is for entertainment, of course. But it also has an unspoken message: a celebration of the people who recognize the importance of preserving the usable past. In a society that is recycling almost everything but garbage, the mood to preserve, restore, and update is catching. Often the impulse is nostalgic. Sometimes it is the result of very personal feelings about decoration. Sometimes it exhibits a love for history for its own sake. Preservation reflects people's need for security in a constantly changing world.

The author of this book was asked to choose twenty houses that were built in "old" California. Since no private residences exist from the state's eighteenth-century history, she chose an adobe from the early nineteenth century to begin her anthology. She picked the Casa Amesti (c.1833–1850s) in Monterey. A good choice; it is an old house in an old town. She made her other selections from more recent houses that are recognized as old. But then she was confronted with the problem of the cutoff date. Where does modernity begin? She chose 1930, which is appropriate. Everything before then seems old, though I must admit that it is a little embarrassing; her last six houses were built in my lifetime!

I don't see how anyone can quarrel with her choices. They are all good examples of their periods. In fact, this book may sharpen your vision and open ways of seeing architecture with close and educated scrutiny. Enjoyable buildings (and many not-so-enjoyable ones!) are all around you. In *Walden* (1854), Henry David Thoreau wrote, "I have traveled a great deal in Concord." He was, of course, referring to experiencing his hometown in Massachusetts. But you can do the same in your own hometown, wherever it is.

Introduction

LAUREN BRICKER

Climate, culture, and landscape—these are the three factors that most directly influenced the California house through the mid-twentieth century. The state's generally mild climate encouraged a laissez-faire attitude toward design. Except for the more extreme desert and mountain environments, there was little need for the house to function as a protective envelopment sheltering inhabitants against the elements. In fact, the opposite was the case: As settlers became acclimated to California, their living spaces were liberated, allowing them to merge with their surroundings. Cultural reference points—both psychological and physical—factored into the shape of the new living dwellings. Landscape more than any other phenomenon made it possible to fuse these conditions into an environment with its own identity. With the benefit of water, agricultural production flourished, and from fragments of European, Middle Eastern, and Asian gardens the illusions of California were formed.

We often forget the formative role played by California's Spanish settlers. Spanish colonization moved northward along the Pacific Coast, reaching Alta California (which encompasses today's California) in the eighteenth century. The Spanish monarchy sought to increase its land holdings and convert Native Americans to Christianity. In order to further their empire, the Spanish established three institutions: the mission church, the military presidio, and the pueblo or town site. The Franciscan Fathers established 21 mission churches along El Camino Real (The Royal Road), from San Diego to Sonoma, between 1769 and 1823.

Mission San Carlos Borromeo de Carmelo, shown here, is but one example. Founded by Father Junipero Serra, father of the California missions, the present building was located at its current site in Carmel in 1793, and it was laid out in a large quadrangle, with the church occupying one corner and the other facilities distributed within the enclosing courtyard. Architecturally, the stone masonry church is distinguished by its asymmetrical composition of bell towers and door and window details, especially the quatrefoil window above the entrance.

Above left: 1996 reconstruction of First Lieutenant's Quarters and Soldiers' Quarters (originally completed 1786–1787), Northeast Corner, El Presidio de Santa Bárbara State Historic Park, Santa Barbara. The reconstructed three-room suite, plus cocina and dispensa of the First Lieutenant's quarters, and soldiers' quarters, were built on their original stone foundations. The Santa Barbara Trust for Historic Preservation, which has been interpreting the archaeology, researching documentation, and reconstructing sections of the presidio for five decades, often uses the soldiers' quarters for ongoing museum installations and a variety of educational programs.

Below left: El Molino Viejo (The Old Mill), San Marino. El Molino Viejo, or "the old mill," was constructed around 1816 to support life at the San Gabriel Mission. Originally a grinding room and granary were on the upper level with large working water wheels reaching into the streams that flowed through the lower level of the sturdy stone, wood, and adobe structure. Today El Molino Viejo is administered by The Old Mill Foundation and is open to the public as a museum and gallery. El Molino is a California Historic Landmark. Photography by Lisa Blackburn for the Old Mill Foundation.

The Spanish built four presidios, or military outposts. The presidios protected the missions and settlers against attack, provided a seat of government, and guarded the land against foreign invasion. The Santa Barbara Presidio (shown here), founded in 1782, was the military headquarters and government center for the region that extended from southern San Luis Obispo County to and included Los Angeles. The presidio was laid out in a large quadrangle that framed the central parade ground, or Plaza de Armas. The most prominent structure was the chapel. This was the first church for the new town of Santa Barbara. One of only two sections that date from the Spanish period is El Cuartel, the family residence of the soldier assigned to guard the western gate into the complex. El Cuartel provides a tangible connection between Spanish settlement and our own time. Its thick walls are constructed of whitewashed adobe bricks, and its roof is covered by red clay tiles.

Vernacular adobe structures are the most significant architectural remains of California's Mexican period of settlement (1821–1846). These adobes were one or two stories in height; often the second story was an addition to an existing structure. Whether on the ranchos or in nascent urban communities, adobes constituted the permanent construction during this period. Low-pitched roofs covered with ceramic tile or wooden shakes sheltered the adobes; access to the interiors was principally under covered walkways or balconies. Monterey is particularly famous for its two-story adobes owing to the large number that have survived and now comprise the Monterey State Historic Park. The versatility of the adobe is evidenced by the fact that essentially the same building type was used for the oldest government building in California—the Custom House (c. 1814–1841)—and for residences—the Larkin House (1834–1838) and the Casa Amesti (c. 1833). These Monterey adobes are the result of merging features from two architectural traditions: the thick-walled adobe construction of Mexico and the Anglo-American use of milled lumber in cantilevered balconies and two-story porches.

By the mid-nineteenth century, regional differences between Northern and Southern California were becoming more apparent. A variety of factors influenced this rift, including demographic shifts associated with the Gold Rush and the related overnight growth of San Francisco. These helped shift the architectural norm toward the range of Victorian-era styles affecting architecture in Chicago and along the Eastern seaboard. Large houses such as the Albert Gallatin House in Sacramento (designed by architect Nathaniel Goodell in 1877) synthesized the fashionable Second Empire and Queen Anne styles. The Victorian "pile" may have seemed old-fashioned when the state purchased it in 1903 to be the official governor's mansion, but its impressive size and convenient location (near the capitol) made its selection appropriate.

Several Victorian-era styles dominated small-town Northern California cities and towns. The Italianate and, to a lesser extent, Gothic Revival comingled with the Queen Anne in the design of speculative and custom-designed houses. This phenomenon is well-preserved in the city of Ferndale. Located in the heart of redwood country, its houses demonstrate the range of architectural imagery that could be executed in wood.

The tenets of the international Arts & Crafts movement—use of natural materials, emphasis on handcraftsmanship, and connection between building and site—were all at play in early-twentieth-century California houses. But in the hands of a number of master designers (Greene and Greene in Pasadena and Bernard Maybeck in the Bay Area, to name only two of the many important firms), using local materials—redwood and arroyo masonry (from the Arroyo Seco in Pasadena)—created a new architecture that formed an identifiable California style. The palette of the Craftsman house included English and Anglo-Colonial variations. The Mortimer Fleishhacker Sr. Estate in Woodside (Greene and Greene, 1911–1912, with later additions) exemplifies a Craftsman interpretation of an English house and garden. The ubiquitous California bungalow brought the Craftsman house to the middle class, and, as

Above right: The Monterey Custom House, Monterey, National Historic Landmark and part of the Monterey State Historic Park. The Custom House in Monterey is the oldest public structure in California. Its architecture changed through the different political eras: the adobe-and-stone structure was begun by the Spanish in 1814, the roof added in 1822 during the Mexican era, and the towers added about 1846 when California came under American rule. It is open to the public.

Belowo right: The Larkin House, Monterey, a National Historic Landmark and part of the Monterey State Historic Park. Thomas Larkin's two-story residence in Monterey, built from 1834 to 1838, borrowed elements from the domestic architectural traditions of the Caribbean, the Mediterranean, Asia, and North America's eastern seaboard. The wood-and-adobe structure contained at least one wooden balcony on the second floor when it was built. It is a well-known example of what came to be known as the Monterey Colonial style.

Left: Victorian streetscape, Ferndale. Ferndale is a small town in northern California that is famous for its picturesque character. The community is composed almost exclusively of Victorian architecture. Fine examples of late Queen Anne, Eastlake, and Italianate style architecture are found in Ferndale.

Below left: The Charles F. Lummis Home (El Alisal) and Garden, Los Angeles (Highland Park), a California Historic Landmark. Charles Fletcher Lummis was infatuated with the American Southwest and its Native American culture. He was an adventurer, an ethnographer, a translator, a collector, and a Native American rights activist, who founded the Southwest Museum and the California Landmarks Club (1895). His Highland Park home, built from 1898 to 1910, is constructed of river rocks from the Arroyo Seco and designed with an Arts & Crafts *aesthetic. El Alisal is owned by the Department of Recreation and Parks of the City of Los Angeles and administered in partnership with the Historical Society of Southern California. It is open to the public.*

Right: The Governor's Mansion State Historic Park, Sacramento, a California Historic Landmark. The Italianate mansion was designed by architect Nathaniel Goodell and built from 1877 to 1878. The State of California purchased the impressive house in 1903. The house became the residence for twelve of the governors of California. This original structure is now a museum house owned and administrated as the Governor's Mansion State Historic Park by the California State Parks system and is open to the public on a regular basis. Photograph courtesy of the Governor's Mansion State Historic Park/ Dave Henry.

architectural historian Robert Winter has written, it became the state's greatest export.

One facet of this place-making sensibility was the Mission Revival in 1896. Another was an outgrowth of East Coast Colonial Revival; just as young architects sketched historic buildings from seventeenth- and eighteenth-century New England, so young California architects, many East Coast–educated, drew the ruinous mission churches and adobes to familiarize themselves with the region and develop appropriate source material for new construction.

Lummis's own house, El Alisal or the Lummis Adobe (Sumner Hunt and Theodore Eisen, and Charles Lummis, 1898–1910), is a fine synthesis of the factors influencing Mission Revival. Located in Highland Park, a Los Angeles district, the house appears to grow out of the Arroyo Seco and its surrounding vegetation. Its walls, loosely referential to the Mission Revival, are embedded with arroyo masonry—small, smooth stones from the riverbed. Lummis was an advocate for Native Americans, an avid collector of their artifacts, and the founder of the Southwest Museum, an important repository of Native American art. Today, El Alisal is the home of the Historical Society of Southern California.

Left and right: The California Building (now the Museum of Man) and the Old Globe Theater, Balboa Park, San Diego, listed on the National Register of Historic Places. Architect Bertram G. Goodhue designed the California Building for the Panama–California Exposition in 1915–1916 at Balboa Park in San Diego. Spanish Colonial architecture of Mexico was his inspiration; the building's facade is one of the finest examples of Churrigueresque detailing in America and the prolific use of colorful glazed tile work elsewhere recalls similar decoration on Mexican churches. The Museum of Man, with exhibitions of Native American cultures, is housed within.

Below left: A Mission Revival detail in Balboa Park, San Diego.

Following pages: The Fleishhacker Estate (Green Gables), Woodside. After Charles Greene (Greene & Greene Architects of Pasadena) moved to Carmel to pursue life as an artist, he was hired by the Fleishhackers to build an English country-style house on 75 wooded acres in Woodside. The residence was completed in 1911, but Charles directed the landscaping of the estate for the next 25 years. Water gardens begun in 1927 featured a 65-foot double stairway leading to a 300-foot Roman pool and a series of arched stone columns that resembled Roman ruins. The estate is privately owned.

By the mid-1910s, California's regional identity was associated with the Mediterranean house and its garden. Its popularity grew following the Panama–California Exposition, held in San Diego between 1915–1916. New York architect Bertram Grosvenor Goodhue was selected to be the fair architect. He was knowledgeable about Colonial Mexican architecture, having illustrated a book on the subject, and had already designed the Gillespie House in Montecito, one of the earliest examples of a Mediterranean Revival house. This experience, along with his considerable architectural reputation, prepared him to design the ensemble of fair buildings. Contrary to the usual fate of fair buildings, those designed for the Panama–California Exposition are well preserved in San Diego's Balboa Park, where many of them house the city's cultural institutions.

The impact of the fair, as well as a growing taste for the simplicity of the Andalusian farmhouse of southern Spain and its applicability to the mild climate of California, conspired to make the 1920s the dominant period for the Mediterranean-style house—in all its variants. Not only were new Mediterranean houses designed during the 1920s, but buildings that survived from the Spanish and Mexican periods were converted to residences. Such was the case for *El Molino Viejo*, or The Old Mill (c.1816, restored 1927).

This book brings the California house up to 1930, by which time modern architecture entered California's architectural scene. Over the course of more than one hundred years, the acclimating process of newly arrived Californians evolved into the "California lifestyle."

Casa Amesti
Monterey, c.1833–1850s

In 1542, Juan Rodriguez Cabrillo explored the California coast, but it was not until 1602 when Sebastian Vizcaino entered Monterey Bay that the land was claimed for Spain. Then in 1769 Spain began a concerted effort to colonize the coast of California, with exploratory expeditions by adventurers representing both the crown and the cross. Eventually four presidios (forts) and 21 missions were established in Alta (upper) California to secure a Spanish presence.

Founded in 1770, Monterey is the site of California's first Spanish Presidio, the customshouse of Spain's major port of entry, and its second mission (the site was moved to Carmel in 1771). From 1775 through the end of the Mexican period in 1846, Monterey was the capital of California and its most important town. When Mexico established its independence from Spain in 1822, Monterey became the leading port of entry for all foreign sailing ships trading with California. It grew from a settlement with a cluster of single-story adobes into a small town of approximately one hun-

dred buildings. Many of these adobes, as well as those of prospering merchants all along the California coast, were remodeled with second stories with distinctive architectural elements, such as wooden balconies, in the decade of 1835–1845. It is well documented that design features of these buildings were influenced by the domestic architecture of the Caribbean, the Mediterranean, Asia, and America's East Coast.

Among the finest adobes both in its classic design and preserved quality is the Casa Amesti, built and occupied by Spaniard José Amesti, one of Monterey's earliest merchants. In 1833 Amesti began to construct a one-story, four-room house. As his fortune grew, so did the adobe, and by 1842 it was one and a half stories with an attic. From 1843–1853 the casa was enlarged to the south, and its second story was completed with wooden balconies on the front and rear. With architectural elements made possible by the availability of skilled labor and milled redwood, the structure was transformed into a stylish house in what is now known as the Mon-

Previous pages:
Left: Casa Amesti, originally one story in 1833, had become a two-story adobe residence by 1842. The Casa Amesti is located within the Monterey Old Town Historic District, a National Historic Landmark.

Right: Frances Elkins and David Adler originally designed the formal gardens in the back of the house. The focal point, a tiled fountain with raised borders, was designed to conform to Adler's original design based on one at the Alhambra in Spain.

Above: The largest room on the second floor is the living room. The room's eclectic décor is that of interior designer Frances Elkins, who saved the casa from ruin in 1918 and restored it for her own use.

Right: Elkins's original furnishings and accessories create a sophisticated yet intimate dining room.

terey Colonial style. The casa stayed in the Amesti family until it was sold by Flora McKinley Duckworth, José Amesti's grand-daughter.

In 1918 interior designer Frances Elkins bought the adobe for her residence and professional showroom. With her brother, the prominent architect David Adler, she restored and remodeled the historic house with modern conveniences. They also designed the Moorish-inspired formal garden and greenhouse within the enclosed adobe walls of the backyard.

When Elkins died in 1953, the house and grounds were willed to the National Trust for Historic Preservation. In 1955, friends and clients of Elkins and admirers of the historic adobe formed the private Old Capital Club to ensure its ongoing preservation. The

Left: Original Elkins-era painted and gilded wooden French bookcases line the walls of the library off the entry hall. A reproduction portrait of the king of Spain hangs at the library entrance.

Right: Upstairs, dramatic hand-painted antique Chinese wallpaper from Europe covers the walls. During the restoration, the wallpaper was carefully removed and then reapplied. A portrait of Frances Elkins hangs in what was originally a sitting room off her back bedroom.

A small bedroom behind the living room with its own access to the back balcony was designed by Elkins for her brother, David Adler.

Old Capital Club administers and occupies the building and has raised millions of dollars for its preservation, including a seismic retrofit in 1995 and a complete restoration of the formal garden in 2001. They have also created a substantial endowment for any preservation needs in the future. The Casa Amesti is used daily by the Old Capital Club membership and is open to the public on special occasions.

c.1833–1850s

1918: Restoration, Frances Elkins and David Adler, architect

1995: Seismic retrofit and restoration, Old Capital Club

2001: Restoration of garden, Old Capital Club

Monterey Old Town Historic District, a National Historic Landmark

Listed on the National Register of Historic Places

Owned by Casa Amesti Foundation, operated under the auspices of The National Trust for Historic Preservation

Administered and occupied by the Old Capital Club

Rancho Los Alamos de Santa Elena

Los Alamos, 1839

The Rancho Los Alamos de Santa Elena is set in a rolling hilly terrain dotted with California live oak, vast stretches of undeveloped grazing land, and the Los Alamos Valley below. It is now a privately owned 1,700-acre working cattle ranch. The centerpiece of the ranch is an adobe house built in 1839 by former neophytes (Native American converts to Christianity) from Mission La Purísima for José Antonio Bonifacio de la Guerra y Carrillo, the eldest son of Don José Antonio Julian de la Guerra y Noriega. The father was Comandante of El Presidio, Santa Barbara's Spanish fort, from 1815 to 1827, and until his death in 1858 he was considered Santa Barbara's most powerful political figure, the town's patriarch, and most influential citizen. He was also one of the wealthiest men in Mexican California—and with half a million acres, one of its largest landowners.

Don José's son José Antonio, born in 1805, was the eldest of 12 children, and though he had married María Concepción Manuela Ortega y López in 1824 and was the father of five children by 1833, he was still living at that time in his powerful father's house in Santa Barbara. José Antonio was elected in 1829 as Santa Barbara's *sincido* (treasurer and public attorney) and in 1832 as the town's alcalde (mayor), but he wished to establish his own household and become an independent landowner. As eldest, José Antonio had hoped to inherit the majority of his father's vast landholdings, but in July 1833, Governor Figueroa overruled local practice and confirmed that Mexican inheritance laws would be enforced in California. This had great repercussions for Californios, or second-generation Californians, especially eldest sons of elite families. According to Mexican inheritance laws, one fifth of a man's estate could be left to anyone he designated in his will. The rest was automatically split between the widow, who received two-fifths, and the children, who divided the remaining two-fifths between them.

Previous pages:
Left: Although modified with a new kitchen addition at the south end of the adobe, the nineteenth-century residence retains its undisputed charm. Simple landscaping leads out to rolling hills studded with oak trees.

Right: On the back patio, carved wooden furniture includes a tiled table surrounded by equipales, *Mexican stretched-hide, curved-back chairs, and a settee.*

Above: In the 1950s, an extensive remodel included the addition of a kitchen, dining room, den, bathrooms, and an extension of the sala, or living room.

Right: In the dining room, a curved China cabinet custom-made in Mexico anchors one wall. Another wall features a seventeenth-century Italian mezzo-relievo (messo-relief sculpture) of the risen Christ and artist Charles B. Schreiber's oil painting A Game of Chess *in a gilt frame.*

In 1834 José Antonio moved to Monterey and became active in California politics as an elected member of the *diputación* (the territorial legislature) and a revolutionary leader in the group of liberal sons of elite families who would become an integral part of California's ever-changing political scene.

Beginning in 1833, when the Mexican government began to secularize the mission system, gradually distributing the now state-owned property and mission lands, individual ownership of vast amounts of land became possible. In 1838 José Antonio was on the *diputación* committee for colonization and vacant lands. In December of that year he petitioned the *diputación* for a ranch, and on March 9 of the following year he answered his own petition by granting himself the 48,803-acre Rancho Los Alamos from lands of Mission La Purísima. By May of that year, it is reported, he was busy building a house and starting his ranch. He would be one of only 56 individuals who would own rancho lands by the 1840s in what is now Santa Barbara County.

These elite families remained in power, becoming the wealthy ranchero society, and continued the traditions and close family

Left and right: The thick adobe walls have been protected with stucco and painted a creamy white for simplicity. Eye-catching, colorful wooden Mexican folk art and a Mexican-style rug as a wall hanging enhance the interiors with the spirit of early California's Spanish and Mexican past.

Following pages: The colorful artwork in one of the main rooms includes paintings of old California themes including Pasatiempo *by Stanley Galli. A restored 1920s Chesterfield sofa and a dramatic, richly dyed, hand-embroidered bed ensemble are also used to great effect. The glazed French doors are a modern addition.*

structure integral to their patriarchal society and Californio culture. Members of the de la Guerra family, including José Antonio, remained powerful and well-connected politically and held a variety of elected offices through the 1860s. José Antonio fathered 15 children, 11 of whom survived childhood. In 1872 José Antonio received a patent from the United States government granting ownership of Rancho Los Alamos. He died in 1878 and his wife in 1885.

1839: Mexican land grant to José Antonio Bonifacio de la Guerra y Carrillo

c.1950s: Restoration; addition of kitchen, bathrooms, dining room, den; sala (living room) extension

1969: Addition of guesthouse, garages

c.1980s: Addition of courtyard, stables

National Historic Landmark

Listed on the National Register of Historic Places

Privately owned

Above and left: After 1983, former owners of Rancho Los Alamos created an enclosed garden patio with integral stucco planters, a stone-and-tile fountain, and a wooden gate with handwrought iron embellishment that opens to the oak-studded hills of the working cattle ranch.

Above and left: Verandas of wood construction run along both the front and back lengths of the adobe house. Rancho Los Alamos was designated a National Historic Landmark in 1970.

Frederick Duhring Sr. House
Sonoma, 1859

The Duhring House has always been a family home. It was built in 1859 by Frederick Duhring and his wife, Dorothea, who had six children, four of whom lived only into the 1860s and two of whom were born in the house. These youngest two siblings, Frederick Jr. and Agnes, would become active members of Sonoma's community in adulthood. Today Fred and Nancy Cline, owners of Cline Cellars in Sonoma, are raising their seven children here. Both the Duhring and Cline families have strong and enduring ties to Sonoma, and with the renovation of the estate, the Clines have not only provided a spectacular house for their growing family but have saved an important part of the legacy of the Duhring family in Sonoma.

Frederick and Dorothea Duhring were newlyweds when they immigrated to Sonoma from Germany in 1852. The Duhrings became examples of those who sold supplies to gold miners and often became wealthier than the miners themselves. Soon after their arrival, Frederick bought a dry goods business housed in an adobe on the plaza (which his son would later raze and replace

with an impressive brick structure) and became a prosperous merchant to hopeful miners headed to the Sierras. Meanwhile Dorothea, who had studied with Franz Liszt, taught piano lessons to General Vallejo's daughters.

In 1859 the successful Duhrings built this large Victorian farmhouse of redwood, a material abundantly available in Northern California, on a large parcel of land near his business. In 1890 the addition of a west wing included a stylish ballroom lit by large bay windows. In 1928 the house became the residence of Frederick and Dorothea's youngest daughter, Agnes, and her husband, Sonoma County Judge Thomas Carmen Denny. The Dennys' extensive 1929 remodel added a Neoclassical entry portico with Doric columns and a formal garden designed by prominent landscape architect Thomas Church. This work transformed the Victorian farmhouse into the popular American Colonial Revival style. The house remained in the Duhring family until 1962, when it was sold and the property divided, leaving 2.82 acres with the main house.

Previous pages
Left: The Sonoma farmhouse underwent a second remodel in 1929 when a dramatic Neoclassical entry portico with Doric columns transformed it into a stylish American Colonial Revival residence.

Right: Facing the entrance to the house is a substantial fountain of Bacchus that celebrates wine and the family's business, Cline Cellars.

Left: A large ballroom with grand bay windows was added as a west wing in 1890. Interior designer Robin Nelson assembled an eclectic choice of antiques and furniture upholstered in rich tones of velvet and damask.

Above: The ornately carved newel post and gleaming balustrade of the massive staircase are among the fine millwork that received complete restoration during the renovation.

Following pages: Much of the interior is embellished with ornate wallpaper from California company Bradbury & Bradbury. The Clines have chosen many hand-silk-screened reproductions of historic patterns highlighted with luster accents.

Above: The formal dining room off the kitchen exudes warmth with its decorative earth tones and well-polished furniture.

Right: Designer Karin Campion created various workstations in the kitchen to accommodate the Clines' seven children's homework at the wooden farm table or cooking in the kitchen. Glazed French doors and windows, a slab of solid white marble for the central working space, and elegant cupboards enhance the lightness of the room.

A few owners came and went before the Clines bought the house and land in 2001 and began a careful two-year restoration and remodel. They chose to raise their family in a historic house partly because Nancy, who has always been interested in history and believes "every place has a story," found it worthy to honor those who went before, confirming the continuum of life. Appreciating the history of a place and feeling responsible to care properly for the land are lessons the Clines hope to impress upon their children. Integrated into their daily lives are the story of this sturdy house and a working relationship with the land. To that end the Clines have planted the backyard with a massive organic vegetable garden whose fresh produce is sold at a local farmers' market. A huge collection of solar panels powers water from an artesian well that feeds the garden as well as supplying electricity to the house.

c.1890s: Addition of west wing with ballroom

1928: Remodel; addition of front porch; installation of indoor plumbing, Bliss & Flaville, Architects, San Francisco

2003: Renovation

2003: Remodel of kitchen, Karin Campion, architectural designer

Owned by Fred and Nancy Cline

Thomas Marshall Dunn House
Victorian Gothic Farmhouse
Sonoma, 1875

Sarah Anderson recalls that in the mid-2000s, every time she visited a friend who owned an old farmhouse in Sonoma, "it felt like coming home." In 2008 Sarah and her husband, Darius, bought that house. The work needed to bring the un-restored nineteenth-century structure into twenty-first-century livability was daunting, but the Andersons knew that they had found what they were looking for: something with character that they could restore and make their own.

The overgrown 5 acres included a barn, outbuildings, and a Victorian farmhouse that was originally part of a 75-acre farm established in 1875 after Thomas Marshall Dunn and his wife, Fannie, had emigrated from Long Island. On the farm they raised vegetables, hay, and apples.

The Andersons bought the house in January 2008 and began major work on it a few months later. For nine months the Andersons lived in the restored loft area of the barn on the back of the grounds while they completely renovated, reconstructed, and remodeled the farmhouse. During the course of raising the main house 8 feet onto piers to create a new foundation, all of the plaster fell off of the walls and all of the windows broke. The structure was brought down to its bones.

Subsequently the owners performed an extensive renovation of the entire historic space while always respecting its architectural integrity. Among other work, they replastered all of the walls, copied all of the plaster moldings in wood, removed and then replaced the plaster ceiling medallions for the chandeliers, and installed floor-to-ceiling windows. Improvements to the house for a twenty-first-century lifestyle involved demolition of an exterior staircase, allowing for a remodel of interior spaces at the back of the house, and the addition of a new wraparound back porch. Although most of the house and grounds still retains its natural ruggedness, the areas adjacent to the house have been tamed and manicured, creating a complementary setting for the farmhouse centerpiece.

Previous pages: Darius and Sarah Anderson respected the historic structure during their extensive renovation and remodel from farmhouse into iconic Victorian estate. A Gothic-style window in the front façade of the farmhouse and a pair of large bay windows are distinguishing features.

Left and right: Sarah uses contemporary pieces mixed with eighteenth-century French antiques to create a lively interior in the double parlor. The refinished wood trim is painted a creamy tone to complement the gray replastered walls.

The rustic farmhouse interiors received a touch of refinement after the major work was completed. Sarah's unmistakable style, taste, and talent resulted in interiors with the right combination of eclecticism, soft comfort, and chic rusticity. Besides owning Ramekins, a culinary school in Sonoma that Sarah has developed to include an inn and an event center, she also owns Chateau Sonoma, a large store with a garden furnishings area that sells authentic country antiques from her regular buying trips to small villages in France. Many of the treasures from her European travels, especially those showing her fondness for French details, work perfectly with the house's neutral palette. Eye-catching details blend with subtle finishes such as refinished dark-stained wood floors, walls painted in gray tones with woodwork trim in a creamy color, furniture upholstered in unbleached linen, and an array of objects from nature. The Andersons' house is an illustration of how picturesque and workable the blending of old and new can be. With a refreshed, relaxed ambiance, the newly strengthened house is a gem worthy of Sonoma's unique heritage.

2008: Renovation of barn
2009: Renovation and remodel of farmhouse
2009: Pool, pool house, spa, garages
Owned by Darius and Sarah Anderson

Above: In the dining room, an eighteenth-century wooden, painted ecclesiastical figure is surrounded by early-twentieth-century California plein-air landscapes. The gilded frames reflect the glow of low lighting in the evening. Above an early-nineteenth-century French farm table, a chandelier made with nineteenth-century parts hangs.

Right: The library's nature-themed décor includes historic books on ornithology and nineteenth-century taxidermic specimens. The French pine with ebonized-wood inlay Directoire-style cabinet holds the collections. The nineteenth-century clock that dominates the far wall is from a train station in Brittany.

Following pages: The breakfast area in the kitchen, decorated with an antique French bottle rack and a picturesque small aviary, has a view of the pool and adjacent picnic area.

Above and right: The Andersons lived in the restored historic barn at the back of the property while restoring the house and grounds. The removal of an exterior staircase allowed for the spacious kitchen and a wrap-around porch that overlooks the beautiful and restrained landscaping of the private estate.

Left: Although the quintessential "San Francisco Style" Victorian that was built in 1886 on a 30-foot-wide lot appears modest in size from the street, its three stories contain 5,000 square feet of living space.

Right: Owner Richard Reutlinger has filled the elegant Italianate architectural gem with collections of mainly American Renaissance revival and Aesthetic Movement furnishings, creating an opulent interior that has been deemed one of the finest Victorian Revival interiors in the country.

Brune-Reutlinger House

San Francisco, 1886

Henry Geilfuss, architectural designer

One of the most well-known, beloved, and authentically restored Victorian buildings in San Francisco is the Brune-Reutlinger House, whose benevolent owner since 1965, Richard Reutlinger, continually opens the house for special events. At these times he shares his vast wealth of Victoriana, including an entire room designated for stained glass–fronted, ornately carved oak, put-a-nickel-in player pianos. In 1973 Reutlinger began a relationship with the Victorian Alliance that has resulted in the sharing of his house, artwork, and furnishings with numerous Victoriana experts, collectors, architectural historians, and lay admirers.

The grand, formal house was designed in 1886 by Henry Geilfuss. Built on a 30-foot-wide lot, its three stories with 5,000 square feet of living space contain ten main rooms and a huge ballroom on the lower level. Reutlinger took nine months to renovate the structure, working mainly by himself, before he moved in. It would be another nine years before he began doing "the fancy stuff," as

he recalls. In the 1970s Reutlinger hired talented craftspeople to restore, reconstruct, and interpret the historic details of the interior. At that time artisans were reviving the techniques so crucial to restoring historic properties, such as fine woodwork, wood graining, stained glass, painting, stenciling, and wallpapering.

The interior is opulent in its interpretation of the period, filled with a fine collection of American Renaissance Revival and Aesthetic Movement furnishings and decorative items that Reutlinger has thoughtfully assembled over more than 40 years. As a teenager Reutlinger began a collection of extraordinary Victorian furnishings that has, through the decades, grown in volume and significance and has converted him into a definitive collector of Victorian-era and Arts & Crafts art and decoration.

The grandly scaled house is a quintessential "San Francisco Style" Victorian defined by a melding of Italianate architecture and Eastlake furniture design interpreted as architectural elements that have been transformed into a vernacular style distinctive to the

Above: An Elkington silver plate epergne from 1858 is the centerpiece on an Eastlake table c.1870s. Rare 1870s shades with a swan motif create a mellow glow of light reflected in the large gilt mirror over the mantel, both original to the house.

Right: The Turkish parlor's atmosphere is created by colorful furnishings, rich fabric, carved architectural wood accents, and intricate Bradbury & Bradbury wallpapers. Treasures include an 1870s horn-and-hide chair, a butterfly lamp, and a brass lamp with glass dome shade bordered with a desert.

Following pages
Left: The ceiling in the morning room/study is a combination of stenciling and wallpaper. The Wooton patent desk is signed and dated 1886, the same year the house was built.

Right: In the main drawing room, a c. 1928 Steinway piano near the bay window supports an arrangement that includes a Spanish glass bust and lithographs in Victorian frames. Nearby is one of a pair of banquet lamps on a Victorian lamp table.

The bathroom on the second floor features Bradbury & Bradbury wallpaper above tiling on the walls. In the Victorian era, the kerosene stove would have provided heat.

Right: An ornate accent to the magnificent c. 1875 walnut bed in the master bedroom is the heavily embroidered silk velvet valance that the owner reappointed from another Victorian house. The small, three-seat ottoman at the foot of the bed is from an old Fox theater.

area. The blending of these styles, along with the Queen Anne, during the 1880s, and the prolific use of bay windows in narrow, vertical, wood-frame house designs created a ubiquitous and now famous style.

After the gold rush of 1849–1853 brought immigrants from all over the world, including trained and experienced designers and builders, to Northern California, San Francisco grew rapidly with row houses and single residences. The majority of these were built quickly, cheaply, and safely using balloon framing with two-by-four wood studs and robustly detailed carved exterior ornamentation. Intricate ornamentation was made possible with the wide availability of malleable redwood lumber and the advancement of equipment such as the jigsaw. Also important were pattern books and such popular publications as Andrew Jackson Downing's *The Architecture of Country Houses* (1850) and Richard Brown's *Domestic Architecture* (1841), which contained explanations on architecture, drawings, and floor plans.

After the turn of the century, new construction in San Francisco moved toward architectural design in the American Colonial tradition, but the numerous houses in the San Francisco Style such as the Brune-Reutlinger House set a precedent in the city and remain iconic in American architectural history.

1965: Restoration
Owned by Richard Reutlinger

Arden

The Helena Modjeska Historic House and Gardens

(Stanford White Additions), Orange County, 1888

Stanford White, architect

The Gilded Age provided wealth to a few fortunate and industrious Americans. In 1878, to serve their building needs, Charles Follen McKim, William Rutherford Mead, and Stanford White formed McKim, Mead & White, considered today the preeminent American architectural firm of its time. During its period of greatest activity, from 1879 to 1915, the firm was awarded more than one thousand commissions and designed some of the most important buildings and grandest residences in the country. A driving force in the firm, Stanford White was celebrated for his genius and, among other projects, he designed summer cottages and luxurious residences for affluent clients such as the Vanderbilts, the Whitneys, and the Astors.

White had been a partner at McKim, Mead & White for ten years when Madame Helena Modjeska asked him to design an addition to the rustic mountain house that she and her aristocratic husband, Karol Bozenta Chlapowski (known as Count Bozenta), now owned in the oak-strewn hills of Southern California. Modjeska, who had been a star of the Warsaw stage, and her husband had moved from Poland to Southern California in 1876 to begin an agricultural enterprise with other Polish aristocrats. During the next few years, as the experiment failed, Madame Modjeska learned English and became a successful actress in America, performing from San Francisco to Chicago to New York. By 1883 Madame and her husband had bought half of the 160-acre Joseph Pleasants homestead in Santiago Canyon and by 1888 the entire property. The bucolic setting, with its creeks, live oaks, and wildlife, reminded Modjeska of the "Forest of Arden" from Shakespeare's play *As You Like It*, in which she had starred as Rosalind; she

Previous pages
Pages 68–69: By 1888, actress Helena Modjeska and her husband had bought all of a 160-acre homestead in the wilderness of Santiago Canyon. She renamed it Arden because the setting reminded her of the Forest of Arden in Shakespeare's As You Like It, *a play she had performed on the American stage. Stanford White's original design did not include the*

bottom row of windows in the front room. They were added after Modjeska's time.

Pages 70–71: A magnificent floor-to-ceiling picture window dominates the architecture of the great room. Paneled bead-board walls and a ceiling stained a natural tint warm the voluminous space.

Above: The massive stone fireplace surround and chimneypiece add visual warmth to the main living space.

Right: Low and stained glass windows and a continuation of the stained-wood paneling create a peaceful atmosphere in the nook used as a music room.

named the estate Arden. Wishing to transform the rustic cabin into a fine house, she chose the most preeminent architect of the day, Stanford White, to make substantial additions.

Today, Elizabeth White, wife of Samuel G. White, great-grand-son of Stanford White, and coauthor, with her husband, of Rizzoli publications *McKim, Mead & White: The Masterworks* and *Stanford White Architect*, confirms that the Modjeska house is included on Leland Roth's list of McKim, Mead & White buildings, which is based on the bill books at the New-York Historical Society. She states, "There is certainly a strong history of attributing this house to Stanford White, but there is probably no documentation. By 1888 White was sticking close to New York City for Madison Square Garden, the Washington Arch, and other projects, so if he designed the Modjeska House, he probably never went to see it."

Madame and her husband lived at Arden for 18 years, though

it was during that time they were often on the road with her acting career. The house was a retreat, a vacation spot, and finally a permanent home. The idyllic Modjeska era ended in 1906 with the sale and subdivision of the estate. Large parcels were bought by the Walker family, who protected the house and woods until they sold them in 1986 to the County of Orange for a historic park. Today the historic estate is open for tours by reservation only.

Date of original house: Unknown

1888: Addition to original house

National Historic Landmark

Owned by the County of Orange, Orange County Parks

George W. Marston House

The Marston House Museum and Gardens, San Diego, 1905

William Hebbard & Irving Gill, architects

George White Marston was a successful businessman and one of San Diego's most influential community leaders by 1905. He and Anna Gunn Marston became examples of steadfast and dedicated public service and influential civic leaders during the important decades in San Diego's evolution from a small town into a modern city. Married in 1878, the couple raised a large family while each also pursued charitable interests. George's perspective encompassed the growing community at large. The confluence of the development of San Diego and the involvement of this exceptional and generous man created projects, organizations, and institutions that have stood the test of time. Among many community projects, he cofounded Pomona College in Claremont and helped establish the YMCA in San Diego.

Marston's particular interest was the natural environment and historic preservation. His work included the preservation and improvement of open spaces for public edification and formal city planning for the growth of San Diego. In 1905 he became the first president of the Park Commission and contributed substantial financial support to create and save Balboa Park. His extensive involvement with the creation of the 1915 Panama–California Exposition at Balboa Park included such duties as chairing the buildings and grounds committee and working as a liaison to the state for funding. He also privately developed Presidio Park and donated it to the city, and for more than 30 years personally sponsored the two plans of San Diego by professional city planner John Nolen. Marston's contribution of strong leadership and generous financial support to his community over seven decades was unequaled.

In 1903 Marston bought ten rough, unleveled acres adjacent to Balboa Park, overlooking a canyon on one side and facing what would become Seventh Avenue on the other. Marston hired the region's preeminent architects, William Hebbard and Irving J. Gill, to design a new house for him, his wife, Anna Gunn, and their five children. He kept 5 acres for his house and formal garden and gave

Previous pages
Left: In 1904, George and Anna
Marston hired preeminent San Diego
architects William S. Hebbard and
Irving J. Gill to design a new house
on 5 acres of hillside bordering
Balboa Park.

Right: The interiors were finished
with first-growth redwood and
Douglas fir with the exception
of the dining room, which is
quarter-sawn oak.

Above: An abundance of interior
doorways and windows creates
a well-lit interior.

Right: The living room is pure Arts
& Crafts and features a seating
arrangement of antique Craftsman
furniture, California plein air art,
and period lighting.

In the music room, a Mission-style upright piano of carved oak was manufactured in Chicago by Price & Teeple. It is of the period but not original to the house. An early photograph of the Marston House predates the estate's landscaping.

Right: The brick fireplace's design, both simple and spacious, is viscerally relaxing. The plaster cast in the over-mantel is a reproduction of a relief by Italian Renaissance sculptor Donatello for a church in Prato, Italy.

Craftsman-style oak furniture and Arts & Crafts ceramics accent the library and complement the finely crafted redwood built-in bookcases.

Following pages: A magnificent built-in oak wall unit in the dining room provides efficient and ample space for gracious dining. The Craftsman-style dining table is set with the Marston family's Haviland dinnerware.

the remainder to his relatives for their houses. Seventh Avenue became a handsome neighborhood with Marston's estate and a series of smaller but well-designed houses in the Arts & Crafts Style, Pueblo Style, and Prairie Style.

The house that Hebbard & Gill designed for the Marston family was an efficient, beautiful, and spacious Arts & Crafts Style design of 8,500 square feet on four floors. The light-filled interior exuded warmth, finished with paneling, trim work, fine built-in cabinetry, and flooring in first-grade redwood. Hebbard & Gill's plan brought the family out of the more formal Victorian era into the progressive future by creating an Arts & Crafts Style house that was a simpler, more functional, straightforward, clean, and spacious design for living.

Irving Gill would go on to become one of the most prominent architects in California during the twentieth century. Until his death in 1936, Gill's designs were led by what Professor David Gebhard described in his essay on Gill for the 1985 *Irving Gill: Birth of a San Diego Style* exhibition catalog as a "puritanical simplicity" and a "passionate Arts & Crafts commitment to the simple life."

The Marston House Museum and Gardens is operated by Save Our Heritage Organisation. Tours available.

Left and right: George Cook originally planned the gardens based on the English Romantic model. The lush garden, surrounded by a brick wall, and the landscaping may be enjoyed today in their full maturity. A Tea House, with tile murals, provides covered seating to the side of the formal flowerbeds and the lawn.

Following pages: The magnificent Marston House, designed by William S. Hebbard and Irving J. Gill, is an outstanding example of Arts & Crafts–style architecture built in America during the early twentieth century.

Henry M. and Laurabelle Robinson House

Pasadena, 1906

Charles and Henry Greene, Greene & Greene, architects

In 1905 Henry M. and Laurabelle Robinson commissioned prominent architects Charles and Henry Greene to design a "simple but spacious" house on 4 acres that overlooked the grand Arroyo Seco canyon in Pasadena. After moving to Pasadena, Mr. Robinson played dynamic roles in the development of such institutions as the Huntington Library, California Institute of Technology, and Mount Palomar Observatory. As adviser and friend to Herbert Hoover, Robinson hosted the president often in the couple's house. The completed 12,000-square-foot residence and carriage house enabled the Robinsons to live comfortably, entertain graciously, and enjoy the ambiance of Southern California.

By 1998, when Phaedra and Mark Ledbetter bought the estate, the house and grounds were in ruinous condition. Their goal was to create a beautiful home within a tastefully designed garden setting and to save an important part of Pasadena, California, and America's architectural heritage. The Ledbetters spent six and a half years living in the carriage house while meticulously and com-

pletely restoring the house, including its infrastructure, and designing and landscaping the parklike grounds.

The Greenes' placement of the house on the bluff provides spectacular views of the grand Arroyo Seco canyon and allows the majority of the estate to remain in open space. The Ledbetters created a landscape that complements the scale and design of the house, integrating wide expanses of lawn, myriad specialty gardens, areas for entertaining, and secluded areas for privacy and contemplation. Noteworthy among an abundant variety of specialty gardens and "outdoor rooms" is an orchard of exotic citrus trees, a lotus pond, a double-helix-shaped *potager*, and an exquisite formal rose garden near the front entrance of the estate.

The Robinson House is one of the magnificent examples of Greene & Greene's California Bungalow Style, built at the height of their most productive period. The aesthetic they developed may be defined by attributes derived from the ideals of the Arts & Crafts movement, the spacious Shingle Style found in houses of the East-

Previous pages
Page 88: The large house that Charles and Henry Greene designed for Henry M. and Laurabelle Robinson in Pasadena is a magnificent example of the California Bungalow style.

Page 89: The front door is impeccably crafted with masterfully carved mahogany paneling and luminous stained glass sections designed by Charles Greene.

Pages 90–91: A breath-taking carved staircase is the outstanding design feature of the expansive entry foyer. Rare Port Orford white cedar wainscoting accents the cantilever-edged stairs and Japanese-style hand rail.

Right: The spacious living room opens to a solarium featuring finely carved Honduras mahogany panels. Owner Phaedra Ledbetter, a California licensed interior designer, furnished the living room to emphasize the Japanese essence of the house's design.

ern seaboard, and Japanese culture and art. Their houses embody a visceral connection to nature through the use of indigenous materials and design that creates a flow between indoors and out and a sophistication from a refined sense of artistry and masterful, fine craftsmanship.

The house is now perfection. The Ledbetters have skillfully brought focus to the fine points of its eclectic architectural influences. As a California licensed interior designer, Phaedra highlighted the more exotic aspects and Japanese elements with her choice of decorative pieces and furnishings, the use of color and texture, and the installation of a whimsical yet practical sushi bar. Not only does the house's interior reveal the unequaled skill and craftsmanship of its designers and artisans in the original woodwork, glass, and furnishings, but it glows again with inner warmth and the spirit in which it was created. The legacy of the Ledbetters' generosity of time, resources, and expertise is a gift that honors the work of Charles and Henry Greene and their preeminence as visionary designers of magnificent, large-scale California bungalows of unequaled craftsmanship and beauty.

2005: Restoration of main residence and carriage house
Owned by Phaedra and Mark Ledbetter

Left and right: Hung from the second floor's ceiling is a magnificent mahogany and stained-glass hexagonal pendant light that is original to the house. It creates a bold statement in the spacious entry as the eye is drawn to the high ceiling of the second-floor landing.

Above: A sushi bar incorporated into the interior design of a gathering room that overlooks the Arroyo is a whimsical design of Phaedra's.

Right: The elaborate pendant light and all of the dining room furnishings are reproduction; the originals are displayed in an exhibit in the Scott Gallery at the Huntington Library and Gardens Museum. The chandelier is raised and lowered by a system of weights and leather straps.

Left: The glass-and-wood cabinet is original to the house. It features painted Chinese carvings that served as the inspiration for the large tile fountain installed near the south porch.

Right: The library features built-in cabinets and a cozy inglenook made of solid white oak. Butterfly joinery details add beauty to the pieces.

Left: The back of the house, built at the edge of the Arroyo Seco canyon, allows fine sunset views of the Colorado Street Bridge and the San Gabriel Mountains. Paths lined with Arroyo river rocks lead to terraced gardens.

Right: The Ledbetters completed a large tiled fountain on the south patio that was designed by the Greenes but never built.

Following pages:
Pages 102–103: The Ledbetters incorporated a water feature with a tree design—using the painted, carved Chinese cabinet in the living room as inspiration—in their fully realized version of the large tiled patio fountain. The tiles were custom-made by Cha-Rie Tang.

Pages 104–105: The entire four-acre parcel that had been abandoned for years was re-landscaped by the owners. The couple created various specialty gardens including a Japanese garden, an orchard, a lotus pond, a woodland tepee garden, and two outdoor kitchen gardens.

Magdalena Zanone House

Eureka, 1908 (and the Domingo Zanone House, c. 1870s)

With the redwood forests of Humboldt County as a backdrop and the Pacific coast on its west, Eureka's core looks today much like it did when it was a booming lumber town supplying building materials for the swiftly growing cities of San Francisco and Sacramento during the nineteenth century. In 1841, large-scale milling operations began to use the natural resource of vast redwood groves along the California coast, and by 1854 the four-year-old town of Eureka had seven mills. Pastoral California was swiftly changing into a mechanized western culture. The architectural style that prevailed in Northern California was born of Yankee tradition and embellished with Victorian ornamentation. Eureka is replete with an astounding array of Victorian residential and commercial architecture that displays every aspect of the ornamental detailing that defines the style.

In 1886, Domingo Zanone, an Italian immigrant and a wealthy cattle rancher, bought three and a half acres in the center of Eureka that had been McKenna's Pleasure Park during the late 1870s. He raised a family of seven children in a house that was probably constructed in the 1870s. A fire later destroyed its second story, and the remaining first floor was converted to a one-story house. After Domingo passed away, his widow, Magdalena, hired local builders in 1908 to design and construct a new residence at the far end of the grounds. It was built in a lavish late Victorian Queen Anne Style with a distinctive onion dome and a large enclosed staircase in the entryway. It is now one of the most authentically restored and picturesque large residences in Eureka.

The Kuhnel family owns the two houses and adjoining lawn, gardens, and mature specimen trees that may have survived from the Pleasure Park era. The large late Victorian house is the residence of Ron and Melanie Kuhnel, and the smaller, now one-story house is the residence of Ron's sister, Betty Kuhnel.

Since buying the house and grounds in 1998, they have educated themselves about the history of the house and its style, learned preservation techniques and resources, and worked with professional historical designers to reestablish much of its original landscape. The large 1908 house is a work in progress, with the

The built-in cabinet with a China closet in the dining room is as efficient as it is beautiful. A walnut dining table and chairs complement the polished patina of the carved redwood wainscoting and fireplace surround.

Right: The entrance foyer features stained glass windows surrounded by heavy, decorative redwood trim that reinforces the wide redwood crown molding and floor trim. A gleaming, carved redwood Ionic column lends grandeur.

Left and right: The dining room is an inviting gathering space well lit by curved windows that incorporate stained glass portions. The view out the wide windows includes landscaping original to the Zanones and a row of cypress trees.

interior returned to its original grandeur with gleaming refinished woodwork, authentic and historically correct lighting fixtures, paint and wallpaper finishes appropriate to the period, refinished original hardware, and doors and windows in good working order. They have employed professional artisans as well as completing much of the work themselves. The Kuhnels' dedication to authenticity has resulted in a historic restoration of the highest integrity. Their efforts were honored in 2004, when the house became the first single-family residence in Eureka to be listed on the National Register of Historic Places.

The c.1870 house has also been renovated by the Kuhnels, with its woodwork, wallpapers (all of which are reproductions of papers found in the house), paint, and flooring finished with historic accuracy by a team of talented local craftsmen.

Selby L. Maloy and A. C. Johnston, builders
Listed on the National Register of Historic Places
Owned by Ron and Melanie Kuhnel

Domingo Zanone House
c.1870s–1886
Owned by Betty Kuhnel

Left, top and bottom: Betty Kuhnel, Ron's sister, has restored the original c. 1870s structure on the large estate that was once the home of Domingo and Magdalena Zanone and their family. Her gardens are included in the original Pleasure Park grounds.

Right: Betty Kuhnel has used authentic reproduction wallpaper throughout her house. Wallpaper in Betty's front parlor is a reproduction of the original wallpaper in the room, scraps of which were found behind the fireplace.

Ernest A. Batchelder House

Pasadena, c.1909

Possibly designed by Ernest A. Batchelder and Louis B. Easton, architect

The Craftsman bungalow built by Ernest A. Batchelder in 1909 faces the Arroyo Seco canyon, the defining geological feature of Pasadena. The house's design of a Swiss chalet in stucco and dark wood shingles integrates clinker bricks and Arroyo boulders into its prominent chimney, tying it to the beautiful natural setting of the gorge and the surrounding live oaks. The house is significant for an interior that is a veritable museum of art tile, with beautiful installations of the work of Henry Mercer and the Moravian Pottery and Tile Works at Doylestown, Pennsylvania, and Batchelder's own tiles produced on site in the backyard studio. Its grounds contain an abundance of picturesque elements, such as fountains and paths, created with colorful glazed tile. The house was the personal residence of Batchelder, a major contributor to the Arts & Crafts movement in America, who wrote for *The Craftsman* magazine and founded the most successful art tile manufacturing company in America during the period from 1910 to 1932. His first ceramic studio is in the backyard.

As the Arts & Crafts movement gained momentum in America, the young Ernest Batchelder studied drawing, painting, and design at the Massachusetts Normal Art Institute, where he earned diplomas in these subjects and in methods of teaching. In 1901 he left his first job at Harvard's summer program in the School of Design and moved to Pasadena to teach at the Throop Polytechnic Institute. Before leaving that position in 1909 to build a house and in 1910 to open his own school-workshop and studio, he gained an education in and appreciation for the ideals of the Arts & Crafts movement and its roots in the medieval craft guilds on visits to England and Europe.

Soon after Batchelder opened his backyard studio, he became devoted to the design and production of handmade decorative glazed terra-cotta tiles. His early efforts met with a positive response, and his company grew with the increased demand for these decorative building products, as construction of Arts and Crafts style, and later Spanish Colonial Revival style, architecture

Previous pages
Page 118: Ernest Batchelder's 1909 Craftsman-style bungalow incorporates painted wood shingles, stucco, clinker bricks, river rocks, and boulders from the Arroyo.

Page 119: The front door of the Batchelder house features decorative details in the Arts & Crafts style. The hand-worked copper mailbox cover designed with a rose theme is the work of Douglas Donaldson, who also crafted all of the hardware in the house.

Pages 120–121: The living room is finished in dark stained redwood and Douglas fir (called Oregon pine when the house was built) paneling with an open-beam ceiling. A frieze is filled with a wallpaper border by Bradbury & Bradbury in the Canterbury Rose pattern.

Above and right: An arrangement of Craftsman-style rocking chairs and sofa provides seating in front of the fireplace in the living room. The floor-to-ceiling tiled fireplace was a showcase for Batchelder's tiles as well as those from Henry Mercer of the Moravian Pottery and Tile Works.

Robert Winter, owner since 1972, has used authentic Arts & Crafts furniture and art throughout the house. A handmade pendant light made by Douglas Donaldson features copper silhouettes of Batchelder's "Birds-in-the-Tree" pattern.

grew in Southern California. He quickly outgrew his home studio and moved the business to a larger facility. His artistic tiles were known for their outstanding quality, handmade and later mold-made beauty, and the inventiveness and variety of designs. Until its dissolution in 1932 during the Depression, Batchelder & Wilson was the major manufacturer of art tiles in America, with showrooms in all major cities. Batchelder's legacy as one of the original tile makers in California includes beautiful installations, large and small, in commercial and residential architecture throughout America.

Today Robert Winter, author, historian, and the Arthur G. Coons Professor Emeritus of the History of Ideas at Occidental College and former chair of the History and History of Civilization programs, lives in the Batchelder House, which he has owned since 1972. His *Batchelder Tilemaker* (1999) is an informative and intriguing study of Batchelder's life.

1910: Workshop/studio and kiln
c.1920s: Guest house and garage
Owned by Dr. Robert Winter

A 1928 garage at the back of the house has barn-style doors decorated with handwrought iron and art tiles. Attached to the garage is a guesthouse that Winter uses as an office and workroom.

Right: A small standing fountain in the backyard was designed using Batchelder tiles. The paired birds in the larger tiles are a Byzantine theme, one of Batchelder's favorites.

Following pages: Brick paths and tiled walls add structure to the landscaping of the backyard and gardens. A 1920 panel at the rear of the house is composed of tiles that were Batchelder's interpretation of Mayan glyphs.

Clarence A. Black House
El Cerrito
Santa Barbara, c.1913–1914

Russell Ray and Winsor Soule, architects

When it was completed in 1914, El Cerrito was the first large estate house in the Mission Ridge area of Santa Barbara's upper east side. In years to come, red tile–roofed houses that would fill this eastern slope facing the town would give Santa Barbara its new recognition as America's Riviera.

The house is a rare and beautiful example of the Mission Revival style. After the Philadelphia Centennial of 1876, Americans began to search for an architectural style that would identify their unique heritage. In the East the revival of Georgian architecture became the most popular style and fulfilled this desire for a national identity. In the 1930s Colonial Revival became the predominant domestic style throughout much of the United States. But in California, that style did not resonate, and architects instead found inspiration first in the eighteenth-century architecture of the Spanish missions. A Mission Revival style represented the California experience, as well as taking advantage of readily available building materials such as stucco, terra-cotta roof tiles, and ironwork. By the end of the 1920s, however, the austerity of Mission Revival had proven limited, and the more ornate Spanish Colonial Revival style as well as those with Mediterranean influences became prominent, especially in domestic architecture.

In 1913 Santa Barbara architects Russell Ray and Winsor Soule teamed up to design El Cerrito ("small hill") for Clarence Alexander Black and his wife, Mary Corning Winslow Black. Mr. Black was one of the founders of the Cadillac Motor Company, and Mrs. Black was an accomplished artist. Ray, a Harvard-educated architect who had come to Santa Barbara in 1908, had previously worked on a redesign for Arcady, a magnificent 70-acre estate in Montecito. Boston architect Winsor Soule had worked in 1912 with artist, authoritative collector, and designer Lockwood de Forest Sr. on buildings at Bryn Mawr College in Pennsylvania.

Ray left Santa Barbara for military service but returned in 1926 to resume his architectural practice. Soule's future affiliations with John F. Murphy (Soule & Murphy) and later T. Mitchell Hastings

Previous pages
Pages 130–131: In 1913, Cadillac Motor Company founder and president Clarence A. Black commissioned Santa Barbara architects Winsor Soule and Russell Ray to design a Mission Revival–style residence in the unpopulated hills above the Mission on Santa Barbara's east side.

Pages 132–133: The estate is landscaped with indigenous live oak, terraced gardens, and plantings that border a lawn at foundation level. Stonework created by Santa Barbara's Italian stonemasons plays a substantial role in the beauty and charm of the house's design.

Above: The house's fortresslike presence is enhanced with a masterfully carved Santa Barbara sandstone foundation. Stones were cut from gigantic boulders that covered the hillsides of the large parcel. This south-facing façade of the house greets the visitor at the end of the driveway.

Right: After 1927, millionairess widow and new owner Hilda Boldt began to drastically change the estate's landscape by adding watercourses, a pool house, a golf course, and a forest of Monterey cypress. She also fundamentally changed the architecture by creating substantial structures on the rooftop level.

Above and right: The current owners hired renowned interior designer John Saladino to create elegant, inviting interiors for the formal dining room and the public living spaces during the renovation in 2002.

Following pages: Saladino carries his theme of dramatically beautiful yet soft design from the grounded blue-gray entry room into the large living room. The carved walnut paneling that was added in the early 1930s gives both formality and warmth to the room.

(Soule, Murphy & Hastings) produced many successful commercial and residential projects in Santa Barbara. Soule's 1924 publication *Spanish Farm Houses and Minor Public Buildings* created an instant classic resource that is still valued by architects today.

El Cerrito's magnificent stonework—the foundation of the house, garden and patio walls, entrance gateposts, and miles of retaining walls on approximately one and three-fourths miles of roads leading up the hill—are exceptionally superior displays of the stonemason's art and a prolific use of indigenous Santa Barbara sandstone. Beginning in the 1870s, Santa Barbara was transformed with new civic buildings, residences, road borders, walls, bridges, and all matter of ornamentation constructed with the abundant, beautiful, mellow-toned, indigenous sandstone. In the teens, those like Black, who had a vision and who could afford superior craftsmanship and design, combined with the skilled second-generation Italian artisans living in Santa Barbara and the indigenous sandstone, resulted in the production of the highly crafted, beautiful stonework so essential to Santa Barbara's unique and world-renowned ambiance.

c.1930s: Additions of pool house, porte-cochere, servants' quarters; remodel of main house interior

1951: Remodel of second floor; remodel of servants' quarters

1974: Property division—5 acres remains with house

1976: Restoration of main residence

2002: Restoration of main residence; remodel of kitchen

Privately owned

Above and right: The residence's terraced gardens and hilltop location provide spectacular views of Santa Barbara.

Following pages: The inner courtyard serves as a patio and reception/ entertainment area. Exterior doors under the arcade lead to each room in the house. Arched terra-cotta roof tiles, thick stuccoed walls, massive wrought-ironwork, and the exterior stonework refer to the materials of the California missions and give the house its solidity.

Smith-Heberton House

El Hogar

Montecito, 1918

George Washington Smith, architect

Originally named Casa Dracaena (after the plant), El Hogar ("The Hearth") was built in 1918 as the residence of George Washington Smith and his wife, Mary Catherine Greenough Smith. In 1917, the Smiths bought 7 acres in the semi-rural enclave of Montecito in order for Mr. Smith, an aspiring artist, to paint. Smith had always been drawn to painting, but as a young man was encouraged instead to study architecture at Harvard, at the time a more practical vocation. Smith left Harvard before graduation and later became financially independent as a successful bond salesman. The Smiths were married in 1912 and shortly thereafter traveled to Europe, eventually settling in Paris, where Smith pursued his career in painting. At the onset of World War I the couple returned to the United States. After traveling across the country, they settled in the Santa Barbara area, where they became a part of the exclusive social set of Montecito.

Smith soon realized that he would never make a living selling his paintings. Instead, his friends showed enthusiasm for the architectural design of his recently completed house, El Hogar. Smith patterned the scheme of his residence on Andalusian farmhouses of southern Spain, the principal characteristics of which are best exemplified by a simplified, almost primitive quality in form, massing, and decorative treatment. This interpretation of Spanish vernacular architecture coincided with a growing appreciation of California's Spanish and Mexican past and the development of the more elaborate Spanish Colonial Revival style, made popular by the buildings at Balboa Park in San Diego for the 1915 California-Panama Exposition.

Smith opened an architectural practice, and within a year of completing El Hogar he had received five commissions. In 1920, he sold El Hogar to his friend, Craig Heberton, and built a nearby

Previous pages
Left: El Hogar's design
is quintessentially Smith:
primitive and simple,
with whitewashed
surfaces minimally
detailed. The popularity
of this residence's design
resulted in a decade of
projects that came to
define the architecture
of Santa Barbara.

Right: Smith often used
glazed terra-cotta tiles
from Tunisia and
southern Spain on his
projects. This decorative
wall fountain is found in
what is now the enclosed
side patio.

Above: A narrow stone
staircase winds its way to
the private quarters on
the second floor. The
stairwell is placed to the
side of the opening
between the main living
room and the large side
room that was originally
Smith's painting studio.

Right: An opening for a
curved hallway that leads
to a guest suite and office
was not part of the
original plan. The
extension, intended for
additional bedrooms,
was added after Craig
Heberton purchased the
house in 1920.

Left: This voluminous room, with its high, open-beamed wood ceiling, picturesque fireplace, and a window that fills the room with northern light, was originally George Washington Smith's studio. He eventually gave up painting for a more lucrative career in architecture.

Right: Designs for the fireplace and niche in the living room are simple, straightforward, and pure. These architectural details exemplify the relatively unadorned Spanish Revival style, the essence of which is found in the vernacular architecture of rural southern Spain.

The formal dining room is located between the large studio and the kitchen. It is a well-proportioned and intimate space with a low wood beam ceiling, a cozy corner fireplace, and a wall of windows that looks out onto the back terrace and gardens.

second house, Casa El Greco ("House of the Greek"), which included a drafting room for his newly formed architectural business. Smith's aesthetic sense, his ability to design structures with proportions and massing that appeared as artful, almost simple cubic forms, and his talent for combining various architectural elements into simple, elegant designs, were evident from the beginning and instantly recognizable. Although he worked in other styles, the majority of Smith's projects evoked the romantic imagery of southern Spain. His work profoundly changed the character of Santa Barbara. This was especially true following the 1925 earthquake, when the town was rebuilt with a Spanish image.

Smith, whose illustrious career lasted only 11 years, is known as one of the greatest purveyors of the Spanish Revival style. His residences, civic buildings, and churches display a restrained, sophisticated, and masterful treatment of the elements found in the vernacular buildings in the countryside and towns of southern Spain, and are elegant interpretations of the Spanish style. His work was greatly celebrated in his lifetime, respected by other Southern California architects, and has endured to the present as some of the finest examples of that architectural style.

1920: Addition of master bedroom suite, office, garage
Privately owned

The living room contains French
doors with lunettes above that open
to the back terrace and gardens.
Smith situated this house, as he did
others later, toward one side of the
site in order to maximize the space
that could be used for gardens.

Following pages: Smith considered
a house's gardens integral to the
overall plan of the estate. He
designed El Hogar's backyard to be
a series of garden spaces. With a
fountain placed as the focal point,
brick paths connect elements such as
boxwood parterres, benches covered
in decorative glazed tile, and a
reflecting pond to recall the
gardens of southern Spain.

Francis R. Welles House

Villa Carlotta

Altadena, 1918

Myron Hunt, architect

Altadena is one of the communities located at the base of the soaring San Gabriel Mountains that typified Southern California as the land of plenty at the turn of the nineteenth century. Fertile soil, plentiful sun, and a moderate, semiarid climate made growing conditions optimal and the good life attainable. Quaint towns in the "Southland" had been promoted from the 1870s in travel journals, tourist brochures, and later in real estate development pamphlets as ideal places to live. Many wealthy Easterners vacationed and later built second homes here. The years between World War I and World War II brought a qualitative change to the area. The agricultural economy became one of urbanization, automobiles demanding more roads became the major mode of transportation, and the population of such towns as Los Angeles and Pasadena exploded. New towns created a multitude of opportunities for aspiring architects.

Myron Hunt was an 1893 graduate of the School of Architecture at M.I.T., where he was trained in the Beaux-Arts tradition. After graduation he studied Renaissance architecture firsthand while living in Florence for more than a year. Upon his return he mainly worked on residential projects in Evanston, Illinois. In 1903 he moved to Pasadena, and by the end of his partnership with Elmer Grey in 1910 he had established himself as one of the premier architects in Southern California.

During his 44-year career in California he completed more than 400 projects, most of which were in Pasadena and Los Angeles. With Elmer Grey, alone, and later with Harold C. Chambers (1920–1947) he built houses, hotels, hospitals, country clubs, schools, libraries, banks, churches, the Rose Bowl stadium, buildings at Throop Polytechnic Institute (now California Institute of Technology), and Pomona College (1908–1930). From 1912 to 1940 he

Previous pages: Myron
Hunt's design for Francis
R. Welles's home reflected
its Southern California
placement and the
architecture of the day,
using design elements
from the Spanish Revival
and Monterey Colonial
styles within the general
California
Mediterranean style.

Left: At the far end of the
library, a six-foot-wide
opening that leads to the
spacious entry foyer and
the front rooms beyond
may be closed off with
pocket doors.

Right: The elegant entry
foyer is dominated by a
grand, wide staircase
made of solid quarter-
sawn oak. The beautiful,
uncommon wood was also
used for the flooring.

*Above and right: The 25-by-30-foot
library, a majestic, quiet space, serves
as the living room. A variety of woods
glow with rich patinas. The floor-to-
ceiling bookcases and paneling are
carved teak and mahogany, while the
doors, window trim, and flooring is
quarter-sawn oak. The oil painting
above the fireplace is by Bay Area
artist Rob Setrakian.*

Gardens that emulated those of southern Spain and Italy were often incorporated into the landscape of houses built in Southern California. Fountains, courtyards, glazed terra-cotta tile, and the use of iron, stone, and stucco were elements that evoked the beauty and aesthetic of historic Mediterranean architecture.

worked on Occidental College, creating the master plan for the campus and completing 21 buildings. The majority of his designs were clean, straightforward interpretations of the Mediterranean style that always considered California's mild climate. He was dedicated to community service and sat on many boards and committees. He was also well connected socially. Although not a rich man himself, he attracted important and wealthy clients, businessmen who appreciated his meticulous accounting for every aspect of proposed designs. He became Henry E. Huntington's favorite architect and built many important projects for him in Pasadena.

Myron Hunt was at the height of his career in 1918 when he was hired by successful businessman Francis R. Welles to build a house on a treeless parcel of land that had panoramic views of the San Gabriel Valley and Mountains. Welles had been asked by Alexander Graham Bell to scout Europe for a site on which to build

a production facility for telephone equipment and bring telephone service to Europe. Welles established a European Western Electric affiliate in Belgium but lived in Paris and in a country house in Bourre, France. Hunt was asked to incorporate elements from the Paris apartment and the country house into his plans for the Altadena house. When completed, the 7,000-square-foot residence had 17 rooms in two stories and included a full basement. It incorporated all of the latest technology and was finished on the interior with finely carved exotic woods. The house became the permanent residence for the Welles family.

1960: Property subdivided
2005: Restoration
Owned by Judie and J. P. O'Neill

Brooks Frothingham House
Las Tapias
Santa Barbara, 1922

George Washington Smith, architect

Las Tapias ("the garden walls") was one of architect George Washington Smith's earliest commissions. Built on a small corner lot in downtown Santa Barbara, it was designed for a friend of Smith's, Brooks Frothingham, with whom he had attended Harvard in 1896. Frothingham, a Boston architect, and his wife, Grace, initially intended the house to be a winter retreat; subsequently, Las Tapias became the Frothinghams' full-time residence. At the time they engaged Smith, he had recently hired a young architectural graduate from the University of California at Berkeley, Lutah Maria Riggs. Riggs became his most valuable employee and a personal friend. Her design drawings, including those for Las Tapias, were rendered with such brilliance that she was considered among the most talented delineators in America. Riggs received her architect's license in 1928 and continued to

work with Smith until his death in 1930; shortly afterward, Riggs opened her own firm, continuing to work successfully in her field until her retirement in 1980.

Las Tapias was designed in the Spanish Revival style and typifies Smith's preference for restrained ornamentation. Drawing inspiration from Spain's Andalusian farmhouses, Smith's houses are characterized by their thick stucco walls, deep window reveals, handmade terra-cotta roof tiles, and sparse ornamentation that mostly included wrought-iron balconies, decorative cement or iron window grilles, and ceramic tile. Like his exteriors, Smith's interiors were relatively unadorned, with ornamentation generally limited to the use of decorative glazed tiles as insets in patterned floor tiles, as doorway surrounds, and as risers on stairs. In all of Smith's work, landscaping was an integral component to his overall design.

Previous pages: A high stucco wall surrounds the George Washington Smith–designed house and gardens built for Brooks Frothingham in 1922. Owners Errol Jahnke and Marilynn Jorgensen have created a welcoming inner sanctum with thoughtful landscaping.

Above left: The entry hall is livened by colorful stair risers that were stenciled to resemble Mexican tile. The stairway leads from the public rooms to the master suite and guest quarters.

Above right: Ornate handwrought iron lighting fixtures, such as the filigreed pendant lantern over the stairway, create dramatic accents against the white walls and add character to the interiors.

Right: The living room to the right of the entry foyer has glazed French doors that face the large, sunny patio and a secret entrance (the bookcase opens as a door) leading to the library/den that was originally a garage.

Colorful glazed Mexican ceramics, a dramatic pattern for the drapery, a dining set featuring a hefty, Spanish-style carved dining table of recycled Brazilian rosewood, and the authentic 1920s iron chandelier and sconces blend to create an intimate dining room with the warmth of Spanish Colonial Revival style.

Following pages: A wall of glazed, bifolding doors opens the breakfast nook to the patio for enjoyment of Santa Barbara's enviable weather. A perfect area for intimate gatherings or large crowds, the patio features a picturesque horno fireplace, styled after those used by California's Spanish and Mexican settlers in the eighteenth century.

With tall protective walls, the inner courtyard patio is private and peaceful, as Smith intended. Owners Jahnke and Jorgensen have honored the historic house by working on its restoration and renovation since their purchase in 2004.

Following pages: The owners are also restoring the half-acre formal garden that Smith viewed as an integral part of his overall design. A Spanish-style stone fountain centers the design as brick paths lead to secluded seating areas as well as a large vegetable garden.

Smith designed the 3,700-square-foot L-shaped Las Tapias to sit close to the corner of two lot lines, providing optimal space for the terrace and garden. High stucco walls that surround the entirety create a private sanctuary and buffer the house from the city's noise and traffic.

In 2004, Las Tapias was bought by Errol Jahnke and Marilynn Jorgensen. As stewards of the house and grounds, their respect for Smith's original design is evident in their sensitive interior remodel. When Las Tapias was featured as the 2006 Design Showcase House and Gardens to benefit C.A.L.M. (Child Abuse Listening Mediation Center) certain upgrading of functional spaces such as the kitchen took place. The owners allowed only changes to the interior that would be compatible with the historic integrity of the house. Whether working in their home offices, cooking together in their renovated kitchen, or entertaining on the tiled patio with its outdoor corner *horno* fireplace, Errol, a real estate broker, and Marilynn, a life coach, consider themselves privileged to be able to live in a house they consider the epitome of the Santa Barbara lifestyle. Today, though modified and enhanced for modern living, Las Tapias continues to convey the charm, intimacy, and design of its bygone past and of its architect, the acclaimed master of the Spanish Revival style, George Washington Smith.

1931: Extension of dining room and upstairs bedroom
1962: Remodel of kitchen and service porch, Robert Ingle Hoyt, architect
1984: Conversion of garage to den; garages, guest quarters
2006: Remodel of kitchen, bathrooms; new patio fountain
Santa Barbara City Landmark
Owned by Errol Jahnke and Marilynn Jorgensen

Sack House and Studio
Berkeley, 1924

Bernard Maybeck, architect (original house and all additions)

When a picturesque 32-acre private estate in North Berkeley was subdivided to form La Loma Park tract in 1907, Bernard and Annie Maybeck bought five lots. They built their first house in that year in what was a sparsely populated, wooded neighborhood in which residents were thoroughly committed to preserving the natural environment and building in harmony with nature. With a growing professional reputation and an eccentric, Bohemian lifestyle, Bernard Maybeck attracted to the neighborhood like-minded, artistic types whose philosophies, tastes, and values reflected the aesthetics of the Arts & Crafts movement, of which Maybeck was a major proponent.

One of the casualties of a raging brushfire that destroyed more than five hundred houses in the hills of North Berkeley in 1923 was the Maybecks' personal residence. Over the next year Maybeck erected a small house on the site that would be fireproof. A friend, John A. Rice, had just patented a building product he called Bub-

blestone that, besides being fireproof, was easily made and cut, malleable, waterproof, lightweight, cheap, and had good insulating properties.

Maybeck used Bubblestone to sheath the new wood-framed house. Wires were strung horizontally, attached to the studs. Burlap sacks that had been dipped in the Bubblestone mixture were then hung, row after row, on the wire. When dried, the sheathing resembled rough shingles in the pale rust-pink color of eucalyptus leaves in the fall, a hue that blended well with the landscape. He would also use the product on his own residence, the Cottage, built nearby in 1926.

Although the original one-room house, known as the Studio, was small, Maybeck's talented use of scale and proportion enlarged the space. An openness was created in the interior with a high wood ceiling and walls of windows on two sides of the room. On a third wall the hearth's rustic cement mantel soared to the ceiling.

Previous pages
Pages 176–177: Architect Bernard
Maybeck built a one-room house
called the Studio on the site of the
larger Maybeck home that burned
in the destructive 1923 fire in the
Berkeley hills. The house was an
experiment in economical building,
using a new fireproof material called
Bubblestone.

Pages 178–179: To create the rough
exterior texture, burlap sacks dipped
in a tub of a mixture of aerated
cement named Bubblestone were
hung on wires and fastened onto
wood slats on the house's framing.
Bubblestone has good insulating
properties, and when dried it could
easily be trimmed.

Right: A high ceiling and walls of
windows on two sides of the main
room make it feel open and
spacious. Current owner Siegfried
Brockmann's fine collection of
antiques includes an eighteenth-
century German polychrome-and-
wood statue of St. Francis Xavier,
which overlooks the room.

Following pages
Left: The front section of the living
room has comfortable seating
surrounded by outstanding examples
of Brockmann's art and antique
collection, an eclectic blend of old
and new.

Right: A large window that looks
out to the back garden frames a
spectacular ensemble of antiques.

The Maybecks' son Wallen lived in the house, used often as a social gathering place for the entire family and friends. In 1926, when daughter Kerna decided to move in, a bedroom and bathroom were added. The house continued to be used for Maybeck friends and family and later included Wallen's wife, Jacomena.

Five of the original houses that Maybeck built for family and friends prior to 1923 on this hillside would survive the fire, and between 1924 and when he retired in 1938, he would build more houses for family and friends, creating a small enclave of like-minded souls.

The houses that the École des Beaux Arts–trained architect designed for himself and his friends possessed the fundamental truths that were embodied in each of his designs throughout his life. His work was sincere, it made use of natural materials in honest ways, and it incorporated beautiful, often ornamented structural members. He strove to create simple designs that directly reflected their functions and worked in harmony with their natural settings. Maybeck was revered in his lifetime for his thoroughly unique, ingenious talent, and he is today deservedly renowned as one of America's most inspirational and iconic architects.

1926: Addition of two-story wing
1951: Second upstairs room with balcony
Owned by Siegfried Brockmann

In 1926, when his daughter Kerna
decided to share the Studio with her
brother, Maybeck added a second floor
with two bedrooms and a bathroom.
A doorway leads from the front office
to a short hallway then down the stairs.

Right: Bifold doors close off the second
bedroom from the first to create two
cozy spaces. Brockmann has used
his collections of books, framed etchings,
and antique statuary to imbue the
rooms with warmth and charm.

William D. Edwards House
Casa Ru

San Marino, 1925

Roland E. Coate Sr., architect

In late 1999, Wesley and Clarisa Ru were enthralled when they first saw the Spanish Revival–style house in San Marino that would become their new home. "We loved the oldness and the integrity of the property," Clarisa explains, "and we also liked the fact that the house was in move-in condition." The 4,800-square-foot house perfectly met the immediate needs of their extended family. The landscaping, however, was another matter. Six-foot-tall boxwood hedges blocked the front entrance view, the driveway was cracking asphalt, and the 2 acres of grounds had not been touched in nearly 40 years. Although needing an extreme makeover, the house and grounds had potential with good bones, mature trees, and enough space for a large vegetable garden.

In the summer after their February 2000 move, they decided to do some firsthand "research and development for the investment," in Clarisa's words, and go to the primary sources of the pictur-

esque California style. Historical roots of the Mediterranean-based California styles (including the Spanish Revival, Spanish Colonial Revival, and Monterey Colonial, among others) are found mostly in Spain, Italy, and northern Africa. So they traveled to Spain, visiting important sites such as the Alhambra and Generalife in Granada, Seville, and the hill towns (their favorite was Rhonda). Also on their itinerary was Marrakech. The couple returned informed and even more enthusiastic about their new purchase.

The original architect for this house, built in 1925 for William D. Edwards, was the talented Roland E. Coate. As a newcomer to California in 1919, Coate began a study of the state's history and its earliest extant buildings, the Spanish missions (or what was left of them), and the adobe houses from the Spanish and Mexican periods. Later, his familiarity with these early California forms, his work on large residential projects with Reginald D. Johnson and

Previous pages
Pages 186–187: The house that architect Roland E. Coate designed for William D. Edwards in San Marino was exemplary of his "simple, sincere, and chaste" Mediterranean designs.

Pages 188–189: The entry foyer is spacious, with gleaming floor tile and colorful glazed tiles surrounding the entrance to the hallway leading to the public rooms. An unusual all-in-one seating piece is possibly Moroccan and features mother-of-pearl inlay work in the highly carved wood.

Pages 190–191: Coate created volume in the spacious living room with a high, open-beamed ceiling. A wide entrance opens onto the hallway with a set of carved-wood doors. Antique handwrought iron andirons decorate the simple silhouette of the fireplace opening.

Right: The flooring pattern of waxed terra-cotta tiles continues down the hallway, leading from the entrance foyer and terminating at the living room, which is set at a right angle to the wide front of the house.

Gordon B. Kaufmann, and his talent and education provided him with experience and expertise that made him one of the most successful practitioners of the Mediterranean style.

His designs were described as "simple, sincere, and chaste," the essence of a style that reflected California's history and environment. In them he grasped the importance of creating residences that would use the Southern California climate to its best advantage and promote the concept of outdoor living. With successful designs that integrated architectural elements such as balconies, loggias, patios, terraces, and courtyards with landscaping that thrived in the semiarid climate, he gained a reputation as an arbiter of good taste and a leader in the design of domestic architecture. He never lacked for commissions from wealthy clients in Southern California, mainly in Pasadena, San Marino, and Los Angeles, and would live in Pasadena, with short intervals living out of state, until his death in 1958. His simple, quintessentially California designs and landscapes create a comfortable informality within private settings that reflect an easier lifestyle imagined in Mexico or the Mediterranean. And his houses continue to be valued and desired for their livability in California's contemporary culture.

1927: Addition of one room to main house, Roland E. Coate Sr., architect

1965: Remodel of c.1925 chauffeur's quarters into new guest house addition

2004: Addition of three-car garage; addition of outdoor entertainment area

Owned by Wesley and Clarisa Ru

*Above and right: Crisp white walls in
the family dining room of the Spanish
Colonial Revival–style house serve as
a backdrop for highly carved, dark
wood furnishings from Revival
Antiques in Pasadena.*

Left and right: One of the changes the Rus made in the restoration was to re-do the back patio. They used the historic bricks to create paths elsewhere, laid new tile, and added a koi pond. The raised border features handmade glazed tiles of Solomon crosses and Moroccan stars.

Following pages: The back façade of the house looks out onto a large portion of the 2-acre estate. The landscape features many areas for entertaining.

Allan St. John Bowie House
Villa Sophia
Hillsborough, 1927

Miller and Warnecke, architects

Villa Sophia, built in 1927 for Allan St. John Bowie, is one of the most historically significant houses in Hillsborough, a small exclusive enclave in San Mateo County 17 miles south of San Francisco. Hillsborough was developed on a portion of land that was originally part of the 6,439-acre Rancho San Mateo, granted in 1846 to Cayetano Arenas of Los Angeles, who sold it that year to William Davis Merry Howard, a native of Hillsboro, New Hampshire, who had immigrated to San Francisco.

This large, heavily wooded portion of the peninsula south of San Francisco was subdivided after Howard's death in 1856, with his wife, Agnes Poett, and her new husband, Howard's brother George, inheriting a major portion. Widowed from George, Agnes married Henry Bowie in 1879. He outlived Agnes, who died in 1893, and inherited the large tract of land that was surrounded by other large estates. The community of Hillsborough developed in the area comprised mainly of second-generation elite families and San Francisco businessmen who wanted to live near to but not in

the city. It was incorporated in 1910 to protect its rural character, and, as a separate legal entity from its neighbors San Mateo and Burlingame, the city gave the residents the right to ban commercial building and sidewalks.

When Henry died, his brother Allan inherited a large portion of the estate's land and money. Allan, who had been an eligible millionaire bachelor for decades, wed Anita Imelda Hughes, and together they built a house in 1927 on 5 choice acres in Hillsborough. The prominent Oakland architecture firm of Miller & Warnecke, proficient in period revival architecture, provided the design that blended an eclectic mix of styles. Allan and his wife were enthusiastic travelers, and treasures from around the world are incorporated into the design. The result was a charming statement with an exterior distinguished predominantly with elements of Spanish Colonial Revival and Italian Villa styles. The spacious 5,000-square-foot interior also incorporates some French and English Tudor influences.

Previous pages
Page 200: The Oakland firm Miller & Warnecke used an eclectic mix of styles in their 1927 design for Allan St. John Bowie and his wife. The front façade successfully combines elements of Spanish Colonial Revival– and Italian Renaissance–style architecture.

Page 201: The ornate plasterwork of the front columns and arches incorporates an element of English design in the Tudor rose details.

Pages 202–203: The entry to the residence is so spacious that it doubles as a reception and entertainment area. Heel indentions in the wood flooring were kept as reminders of various owners through the years. The immense gate that celebrates the living room's entrance is solid bronze from Italy.

Left: Intricate and unusual hand-wrought ironwork designs that are found throughout the house, such as this sconce, original to the house, define the interiors and give them extraordinary character.

Right: Walnut paneling in an English Renaissance style and a ceiling decorated with a honeycomb pressed-plaster motif, often used in the great halls of English manor houses, complete the ode to English Tudor design that the Bowies intended.

Let: An arcade with Gothic-style arches that leads from the house to the garages appears as a cloister.

Right: A guesthouse with its own enclosed, walled patio and an office above were additions of the Scripps family, the second owners of the house. Sets of French doors and a decorative iron gate lead to the back terrace.

Following pages: Thomas Church had designed the original landscape plan for the estate; the Nelsons hired talented Hillsborough landscape architect Lisa Keyston to renovate the overgrown grounds of the estate using portions of Church's design.

By 1938 most of the large estates in Hillsborough had been divided into smaller parcels, and the town of 6.2 square miles had tripled its population to around 2,500, but the rural atmosphere remained, with roads winding through the wooded hills. The Bowies' villa was reputed to be the most spectacular "party" house in the area where, for many decades, various owners entertained lavishly.

In the late 1980s, however, the house fell into decline. When the current owners, Zachary and Elizabeth Nelson, first saw the house in 2007, it was barely visible through heavy overgrowth. Inside they found a well-built structure that had become a dilapidated ruin. To them, however, this was a diamond in the rough. Soon after purchasing the house and grounds in 2008 they began an intense, two-year restoration that not only brought the house back to immaculate condition but allowed a community of creative craftspeople who appreciated the fine details of the historic house to enthusiastically and joyfully participate in bringing it back to life.

2009: Restoration of house and guest house; remodel of pool house into office

Owned by Zachary Nelson and Elizabeth Horn Nelson

Dickinson House
Mariposa
Montecito, 1929
Sidney Stacey, architect

The Dickinson House was designed in 1929 by architect Sidney Stacey, who had earlier worked briefly in the newly formed architectural practice of George Washington Smith. It was designed in the Spanish Revival style that Smith espoused and shows many similarities to his work. Save for the formality of the plaster detailing of the door surround, the large planar surfaces of the front facade and its uniformity of roofline resemble an Andalusian farmhouse, much like Smith's own first residence in Montecito, El Hogar. The building is set similarly close to the street so that a majority of the 6-acres may be appropriated for landscaping. The dramatic courtyard around which Stacey's U-shaped house is built opens to the sweeping back lawn surrounded by lush gardens.

In 2004 Helene Aumont, the interior designer for the house, planned the restoration of the gardens, incorporating traces of the original plan by 1920s Santa Barbara landscape architect Lockwood de Forest Jr. Aumont designed the gardens as she did the house—with the clients in mind. Because the house would be a family retreat but would also be shared on special occasions with extended family and close friends, the interiors and the landscaping had to be user-friendly. A vast lawn anchors the backyard with an orchard, and specialty gardens add interest and glamour.

For a romantic touch, Aumont planned to reconstruct the former greenhouse, but the owners wanted a place that would be more useful for frequent, intimate gatherings. With that in mind, Aumont created an outdoor room with a Moorish essence using the foundation pad of the original greenhouse. The space is magical.

The homeowners are a couple whose good taste leans toward a traditional, Old English style. But Aumont was thrilled to learn that her sophisticated clients also had a hip and completely original approach to color, furnishings, and textures. The designer con-

Previous pages
Pages 210–211: Architect Sidney Stacey designed Mariposa in 1929. The restrained and elegant Spanish Revival–style architecture includes façades punctuated with window openings, ornate handwrought ironwork consisting of well-placed lighting fixtures, window grilles, balconies, and a simplified Neoclassical plaster design surrounding the front door.

Pages 212–213: The house and a back terrace are elevated with a carved Santa Barbara limestone retaining wall. In 2004 Helene Aumont, the interior designer for the house, planned the restoration of the gardens, incorporating traces of 1920s Santa Barbara landscape architect Lockwood de Forest Jr.'s original plan.

Above: Aumont draws attention to one corner of the living room with a spectacular sixteenth-century Spanish vargueño *(folding desk) with intricate marquetry work of painted and gilt wood and inlaid ivory.*

Right: Striking chartreuse paint and gold gilt trim work creates a bold, sophisticated look in the living room. A pair of high built-in niches hold eighteenth-century Spanish polychrome-and-painted-wood angels on either side of the Ely de Vescovi painting above the mantel.

An eighteenth-century Spanish walnut dining table seats twelve. Guests dine by the candlelight of a Venetian eighteenth-century iron and hand-blown glass chandelier while a seventeenth-century Spanish Colonial polychrome-and-wood angel looks on. A spectacular late-sixteenth-century sterling silver repousse retablo depicting paradise and hell hangs on the wall.

firms that their house is a reflection of them—fun-loving, playful, and full of life. Aumont's well-balanced blend of eighteenth-century Italian and French antiques and paintings with contemporary pieces gives the rejuvenated house its unique spirit. A bold chartreuse paint for the living room creates a striking background to highlight the gilded and finely carved decorative collections yet speaks pure modernity when coupled with the newer furnishings. Walls in the dining room frescoed a deep terra-cotta exude a generous feeling of warmth, while the original plaster molding that raises the perceived horizon level and the low ceiling work together advantageously to create coziness. The effect is perfected with candlelight from the Venetian chandelier. For the sunny private quarters upstairs, brightly colored upholstery adds punch to the striking white walls, decorated, as are the halls, with only small eighteenth-century Italian and South American landscapes and antique wrought-iron sconces. The house is now a reflection of its owners with its hip colors, liveliness, élan, and chic style.

2004: Renovation; kitchen remodel, Helene Aumont, designer
Privately owned

Above: One of the specialty gardens Aumont planned is the succulent and cactus garden.

Right: The Moorish-inspired garden is a magical place. Located not far from the house, it is reached by following one of the meandering paths of stepping stones created from Santa Barbara sandstone.

Following pages: An inner garden courtyard is created at the back of the house by three two-story façades. Low, minimal lighting, plain whitewashed walls, and manicured landscaping create a peaceful setting.

J. Henry Behrens House
Cuatro Vientos

Santa Barbara, 1929

Reginald D. Johnson, architect

In 1929 prominent Pasadena and Los Angeles architect Reginald D. Johnson designed Cuatro Vientos ("House of the Four Winds"), for J. Henry Behrens. Johnson's gracious personal manner and his reputation for elegant, carefully detailed designs won him many large residential commissions in Santa Barbara and Montecito during the teens and twenties. As with all of his projects, Johnson paid great attention to advantageously siting the house within the given topography. Accordingly, this elegant Spanish Colonial Revival–style house is set on 3.25 acres of Santa Barbara's Mission Ridge and has a commanding view of the town and the Pacific Ocean from the backyard and a pleasant view of the nearby live oak–studded California landscape and distant foothills from the front of the house. Prominent Santa Barbara landscape architect Ralph T. Stevens designed the grounds. They include impressive trees imported from all over the world, cacti and succulent gardens, a formal rose garden with marble gazebo,

and stone seating among paths set in the side of the hill on the edge of the backyard.

The residence is grandly scaled and was intended to hold Behrens's immense collection of museum-quality fifteenth-, sixteenth-, seventeenth-, and eighteenth-century Spanish and Italian antiques and furniture. Its craftsmanship and materials are of the highest quality, including fine cedar woodwork, oak or terra-cotta tile flooring, decorative paneled ceilings, and carved antique doors. Although the house was built in 1929, its Mediterranean style with elements of the Monterey Colonial, a floor plan that includes a large loggia for outdoor living, and the general feeling of spaciousness are all conducive to the contemporary Southern California lifestyle.

Reginald D. Johnson, F.A.I.A. (Fellow of the American Institute of Architects), was born in New York and received degrees from Williams College and the Massachusetts Institute of Technology. In

Previous pages

Left: The house that architect Reginald D. Johnson designed in 1929 for J. Henry Behrens is a distinctive and elegant interpretation of the Spanish Colonial Revival architectural style. It is grandly scaled and was intended to hold Behrens's vast collection of antique art and furniture.

Right: An ornately carved antique wood chest, marble-topped tables, and elaborate antique gilt frames are stunning accents in the cavernous whitewashed hallway.

Left: Original decorative handwrought iron doors flanked by painted and gold gilt Gothic-style wall plaques create a celebrated entry to the sunken living room.

Right: The entry atrium has a sturdy terra-cotta tile floor and features a massive wooden staircase to the wide landing above. Hefty handwrought iron accents and decorative woodwork seen in the carved columns give the space weight and character.

Previous pages: The sunken living room is made more intimate by a low ceiling whose beams and honeycomb molding has been decoratively painted. Two nineteenth-century Italian seascapes are hung in wood and gilt frames to the left of the fireplace.

Left: The dining room is spacious enough for a variety of seating arrangements. An Andalusian painting in an ornate frame and draperies of rich red embroidered fabric give the room a feeling of old Spain. The marble mantle is dated 1580 and signed "E. L. Ween HR."

Right: A new addition to the house is a handblown glass window that creates its own art.

Left: Original handwrought iron lighting fixtures such as this elaborate dragon sconce are evocative reminders of the fine craftsmanship of artisans working in California during the late teens and 1920s.

Right: The Spanish-inspired back terrace, with its handmade glazed tile wainscoting, stained-wood ceiling, and long arcade, is a beautiful, spacious area for entertaining or just enjoying the panoramic view of Santa Barbara and the Pacific Ocean beyond.

Following pages
Pages 232–233: The house is advantageously sited on Santa Barbara's Mission Ridge. Close to the back terrace, colorful bougainvilleas, iceberg roses, and fragrant night-blooming jasmine form a border that leads to a vast lawn with a swimming pool.

Pages 234–235: From the entry gate a driveway leads to an auto court surrounded by mature plantings that include king and queen palms, succulent gardens, a formal rose garden, and a center island of lawn among palm trees. Johnson celebrated the entrance with a carved stone surround and engaged columns that give the entry vestibule a dramatic presence.

1912 he opened an architectural practice in Pasadena. From 1922 to 1924 he worked in partnership with Gordon B. Kauffmann and Roland E. Coate Sr., each of whom went on to become a prominent Southern California architect. From 1925 until his retirement in 1938 Johnson maintained a high-profile career, in which his work won numerous prestigious awards and was wellpublicized in professional and popular magazines. From his earliest commissions Johnson demonstrated an ability to successfully combine a precise business sense and a masterful skill in designing sophisticated and refined buildings. Johnson's great body of work defined California regionalism. His restrained, elegant designs for residential and public projects would change the look of Southern California's built environment and help to popularize a Mediterranean style that drew heavily from historical precedents of Spanish and Italian country houses. In capturing the romance of the wildly popular Spanish Colonial Revival style with an unequaled elegance, his work is an enduring and striking presence in Santa Barbara.

Although he became one of the most prominent and well-respected architects practicing in Southern California, from the mid-1930s until the end of his life, he focused his attention on affordable housing in Los Angeles. Leaving his upscale residential practice, he devoted himself to this cause.

c.1960: Pool addition
Privately owned

Interior designer Helene Aumont enjoys the country life at her Pepper Hill Farm in the Santa Ynez Valley. The secluded wooden farmhouse and stable rest in a rural setting of six acres of oak-studded hills.

Pepper Hill Farm

Ballard (Santa Ynez Valley), c.1929

Who would guess that Helene Aumont, who grew up in Paris's Sixteenth Arrondissement, modeled haute couture for years, designed her own clothing line, owned an antique import business, has been a sought-after interior designer for 15 years, and for the past ten years designed a line of furniture that is carried in her showrooms across America, would love farming. Actually gardening. And animals. Especially horses. For Aumont, a connection to nature is integral to her philosophy of life. The 400-acre ranch in Corsica that her parents bought when she was six enabled her, as a young person, to experience the freedom of the countryside in a "bowl of fresh air," as she describes it. She spent three months each summer and every holiday there. Whereas the family home in Paris was a *hôtel particulier* with a charming garden, the expansive ranch in Corsica included an old farmhouse, farm animals, vineyards, olive groves, and orchards. Having been a sophisticated city dweller, Aumont has a fine appreciation for nature and now prefers the beauty and casualness of country life.

*Above and right: The cozy home's living
room with stone fireplace surround and
mantel, low seating, and walls hung
with Aumont's favorite art provides
a welcoming retreat from busy city
business and a sanctuary that is
Aumont's personal space.*

Aumont lives a European lifestyle today at her 6-acre Pepper Hill
Farm in the Santa Ynez Valley. A former competitive driver of American Saddlebreds in "fine harness classes," she now keeps two
Friesians and rides them strictly for pleasure. Besides trail rides, she
has built an outdoor riding arena for dressage. On the lower
grounds, surrounded by pastures, Aumont restored a four-stall barn
with tack room and office that she outfitted with antiques and pho-
tos of herself and her children. Small, comforting animals—her dogs
and cats—roam freely, enjoying their country existence.

Her once-barren hilltop is now dominated by lush gardens that
exude an earthy, casual spirit. Between the wooden farmhouse and
office/studio building there is a rose garden, and in the backyard,
overlooking the riding ring, a thriving vegetable garden. Trees
among the gardens have matured since she bought the farm in
1994, and the changes to the house, such as the enclosure and
extension of the front porch into a living space, have transformed
the "sad little house," as Aumont describes it, into a spacious, welcoming home.

Previous pages: Aumont's use and arrangement of unusual eighteenth-century French painted country furniture is masterful. The luscious, antique furnishings help to create an atmosphere conducive to the many intimate and lively conversations that have occurred here through the years.

Right: The back sleeping porch has an ethereal quality, with fabric walls and awnings stretched overhead. From this serene setting there are views out to the vegetable garden and down the hillside to the riding ring and stable.

This is Aumont's refuge and home base to which she returns from travel far and wide, for international as well as domestic business. This is where she lives with her youngest daughter in a European lifestyle close to nature and where she is visited by her two eldest children, a private chef, and an assistant who work in Hollywood. It is here that Aumont takes time to cook and to sit and share good conversation over dinner every night—she designed the kitchen and dining area in the 3,700-square-foot, four-bedroom house to be conducive to this kind of interaction. The veranda and adjoining living room are also places of ultimate relaxation. The Aumont home is full of life. Though it is beautiful, it is comfortable, livable, and, above all, real.

2002: Remodel, Helene Aumont, designer
Owned by Helene Aumont

Left: Aumont has integrated French antiques, wooden pieces with chipped paint and unmistakable patina, into her home's evocative décor. A pair of eighteenth-century Venetian painted and gilded carved wood doors were installed at the entry to the main bedroom.

Right: Beside a painted wood-and-metal altarpiece with gilded, carved wood tassels is artist Marie Laurencin's image of ballerinas in a carved gilded-wood frame.

Previous pages: A deck at the side of the 3,500-square-foot house was widened, and sets of floor-to-ceiling doors and windows with draperies were installed to create an open space to gather in any weather or time of day. The long room has a country flair, with horseshoes lining the walls, casual dining and seating areas, and a profusion of plants on French garden tables.

Left and right: On the lower level of the farm, a stable has two horse stalls and a tack room whose walls display show ribbons and family photographs. Although a former competitor, Aumont now rides her two Friesians simply for pleasure. In this European-style household chickens, cats, and visiting small animals are free to wander.

Acknowledgments

My special thanks go to Paul Rocheleau, the photographer with whom I enjoyed sharing the California I know and love, who brought these historic houses to life with his vivid photography. To Rizzoli editor Douglas Curran, with whom it is always a pleasure to work and who followed the book's development with enthusiasm; to associate publisher David Morton, whose expertise is always invaluable and whose friendship is much appreciated; and to Abigail Sturges, the talented designer who created a beautiful, cohesive book out of many parts.

My thorough gratitude goes to Robert Winter, the Arthur G. Coons Professor Emeritus of the History of Ideas at Occidental College and former chair of the History and History of Civilization programs, renowned historian, and author who graciously agreed to write the foreword, the result of which is delightful and illuminating.

Also special thanks goes to architectural historian Lauren Weiss Bricker, Associate Professor of Architecture, Director, ENV Archives-Special Collection at California State Polytechnic University, Pomona, for her expertise and for her interesting and informative introduction, which gives an easily understandable look into an explanation of California's architectural legacy.

Thanks go to each of the homeowners, curators of house museums, and estate managers, who freely shared their knowledge and made the buildings accessible. I would also like to especially thank professionals in the field of architectural history who shared their expertise: Anthony Bruce, Director of the Berkeley Architectural Heritage Association; Patricia Gebhard, author and architectural historian, Santa Barbara; and Louise Pubols, Chief Curator of History at the Oakland Museum of California.

My thanks also go to realtors Jo Ann Mermis and Wes St. Clair of Prudential California Realty in Montecito for their friendliness, knowledge, and support.

And, of course, my thanks to:

Eli and Laura Adler, San Anselmo
James B. "Beach" Alexander, author, Sonoma
Suzanna Allen, San Francisco
Arcadia Studio (landscape design), Santa Barbara and Phoenix
Arden, The Helena Modjeska Historic House and Gardens: Leslie Ray; Sue McIntire; Tom Starnes; Doug Witherspoon; Gina Drury
Helene Aumont, interior designer, Ballard, San Francisco, Los Angeles, New York

Anthony Bruce, Director, Berkeley Architectural Heritage Association
Bob Burchit, Arcata
Karin Campion, architectural designer, Sonoma
Donna Craig, Academic Personnel, History Dept., University of California, Santa Barbara
Robert and Leslie K. Demler, Sonoma
John and Kathy Ford, Arcadia
Donna and Bob Gafford, owners, Cornelius Daly Inn, Eureka
Patricia Gebhard, author, Santa Barbara
Terri Geis, Preservation Director, Pasadena Heritage
Giffin and Crane General Contractors, Inc., Santa Barbara
Danna Gunther, Encinitas
Margot Hirsch, San Francisco
Cecily Hughes (interior design), Telluride, Colorado
Humboldt County Historical Society, Eureka
Skip Keyzers, Old Capital Club, Monterey
Heather King, San Francisco
Korpinen-Erickson, Inc. (interior design), Santa Barbara
Carter Lowrie, San Francisco
Joanne McIlwraith, San Francisco
Shauna Mika, Mountain View
Monterey County Historical Society, Salinas
Pat Murphy, author, Santa Ynez
Paysage, Inc. (landscape management, construction, consultation), Santa Barbara
Pamela Post, architectural historian, Santa Barbara
Louise Pubols, Chief Curator of History, Oakland Museum of California, Oakland
Revival Antiques, Pasadena
William Ryan, San Francisco
Carol, Bill, and Fiona Ryder, Arcata
San Diego Historical Society, San Diego
Santa Barbara Trust for Historic Preservation: Mike Imwalle, archaeologist; Kendra Rhodes, public affairs and communications
Save Our Heritage Organisation, San Diego
Diane Moll Smith, Manager/Research, Depot Park Museum, Sonoma Valley Historical Society, Sonoma
The Kitchen Company, Santa Barbara
Kathleen Thorne-Thompson, Pasadena
Robert Winter, author, professor, Pasadena
Karin Young, San Francisco

Resources

Alexander, James Beauchamp, and James Lee Heig. *San Francisco: Building the Dream City*. San Francisco: Scottwall Associates, 2002.

Beebe, Rose Marie, and Robert M. Senkewicz, ed. *Lands of Promise and Despair: Chronicles of Early California*, 1535–1846. Santa Clara, California: Santa Clara University and Berkeley, California: Heyday Books, 2001.

Beresford, Hattie. "The Way It Was: Extreme Makeover at El Cerrito," *Montecito Journal*, Vol. 15, Issue 17, April 30–May 7, 2009.

Bricker, Lauren Weiss. *The Mediterranean House in America*. New York: Abrams, 2008.

———. *Johnson, Kaufmann, Coate: Partners in the California Style*. Claremont, California: Trustees of Scripps College, 1992.

Bruce, Anthony, ed. *Maybeck Country: Hillside Houses of the Early- and Mid-20th Century*. Berkeley, California: The Berkeley Architectural Heritage Association, 2009.

Christman, Florence. *The Romance of Balboa Park*. Reprint: San Diego, California: San Diego Historical Society, 1999.

Clark, Alson. "Reginald D. Johnson: Regionalism and Recognition," Bricker, Lauren Weiss. *Johnson, Kaufmann, Coate: Partners in the California Style*. Claremont, California: Trustees of Scripps College, 1992.

Clark, Alson, Peter de Bretteville, and Stefanos Polyzoides, ed. *Myron Hunt, 1868–1952: The Search for a Regional Architecture*. Pasadena, California: Baxter Art Gallery, California Institute of Technology, 1984.

Conrad, Rebecca, and Christopher H. Nelson. *Santa Barbara: A Guide to El Pueblo Viejo*. Santa Barbara, California: Capra Press, 1986.

Dunn, Jerry Camarillo. *The Biltmore, Santa Barbara: A History*. Santa Barbara, California: Albion Publishing Group, 1990, 1996.

Fish, Peter. "Actress in Arden—estate of actress Helena Modjeska in Orange County, California," *Sunset Magazine*, May 2000.

Garrison, G. Richard, and George W. Rustay. *Early Mexican Houses: A Book of Photographs & Measured Drawings*. Stamford, Connecticut: Architectural Book Publishing Co., Inc., (copyright 1930), 1990.

Gebhard, David. *Santa Barbara: The Creation of a New Spain in America*. Santa Barbara, California: The University Art Museum, Santa Barbara, 1982.

———. "The Spanish Colonial Revival in Southern California (1895–1930)," *Journal of the Society of Architectural Historians,* Vol. XXVI, No. 2, May 1967.

Gebhard, David and Harriette Von Breton. *1868: Architecture in California*. Santa Barbara, California: The Regents, University of California, 1968.

Gebhard, David and Robert Winter. *Architecture in Los Angeles: A Compleat Guide*. Salt Lake City: Gibbs M. Smith, Inc. Peregrine Smith Books, 1985.

Gebhard, David, Robert Winter, et al. *The Guide to Architecture in San Francisco and Northern California*. Salt Lake City: Peregrine Smith Books, 1973, 1976, 1985.

Gutierrez, Ramon A. and Richard J. Orsi. *Contested Eden: California Before the Gold Rush*. (Published as Vol. XLLVI, No. 2 and 3 of *California History*, the magazine of the California Historical Society) The University of California Press, 1997.

Hannaford, Donald R., and Revel Edwards. *Spanish Colonial or Adobe Architecture of California, 1800–1850*. Stamford, Connecticut: Architectural Book Publishing Co., Inc., (copyright 1931), 1990.

Heckman, Marlin L. *Santa Barbara American Riviera*. Charleston, South Carolina: Arcadia Publishing, 2000.

Hoover, Mildred Brooke, Hero Eugene Rensch, Ethel Grace Rensch, and William N. Abeloe. Revised by Douglas E. Kyle. *Historic Spots in California*. Stanford, California: Stanford University Press, 2002.

Kennedy, Roger G. *Mission: The History and Architecture of the Missions of North America*. Boston, New York: Houghton Mifflin Company, 1993.

Kirker, Harold. *California's Architectural Frontier: Style and Tradition in the Nineteenth Century*. San Marino, California: The Huntington Library, 1960; Salt Lake City: Gibbs M. Smith, Inc., 1988.

Kurillo, Max and Erline Tuttle. *California's El Camino Real and Its Historic Bells*. San Diego, California: Sunbelt Publications, Inc., 2000.

Lemke, Nancy. *Cabrillo: First European Explorer of the California Coast*. San Luis Obispo, California: EZ Nature Books, 1991.

Newcomb, Rexford. *Spanish-Colonial Architecture in the United States*. New York: J. J. Augustin, 1937; New York: Dover Publications, 1990 (republication of original); New York: Acanthus Press, 1999.

Newland, Joseph N., ed. *Johnson, Kaufmann, Coate: Partners in the California Style*. Claremont, California: Trustees of Scripps College, 1992.

Nicholson, Loren. *Rails Across the Ranchos*. Fresno, California: Valley Publishers, 1980.

Nunis Jr., Doyce B., editor. *From Mexican Days to the Gold Rush: Memoirs of James Wilson Marshall and Edward Gould Buffum Who Grew Up with California.* Chicago: The Lakeside Press, R. R. Donnelley & Sons Company, 1993.

Olmsted, Frederick Law. *The Cotton Kingdom: A Traveller's Observation on Cotton and Slavery in the American Slave States.* Reprint: New York: Alfred A. Knopf, 1953.

Parmelee, Robert D. *Pioneer Sonoma.* Sonoma, California: The Sonoma Valley Historical Society, 1972.

Pourade, Richard F. *The Call to California: The Epic Journey of the Portola-Serra Expedition in 1769.* San Diego, California: The Union-Tribune Publishing Company, 1968.

Pubols, Louise. *The Father of All: The de la Guerra Family, Power, and Patriarchy in Mexican California.* Berkeley, California: University of California Press and San Marino, California, the Huntington Library, 2009.

Robbins, Millie. "The Bowie Estate—What Tales It Has to Tell," *San Mateo County Times.* San Mateo, October 21 and 28, 1983.

Smith, Bruce. *Greene & Greene Masterworks.* San Francisco: Chronicle Books, 1998.

Soule, Winsor. *Spanish Farm Houses and Minor Public Buildings.* New York: Architectural Book Publishing Co., 1924.

Spaulding, Edward Selden. *A Brief Story of Santa Barbara.* Santa Barbara, California: Pacific Coast Publishing Co., 1964.

Starr, Kevin. *California: A History.* New York: Modern Library, an imprint of Random House, Inc., 2005.

Tompkins, Walker A. *Santa Barbara's Royal Rancho: The Fabulous History of Los Dos Pueblos.* Goleta, California: Dos Pueblos Publications, 1987.

Trapp, Kenneth R., et al. *The Arts and Crafts Movement in California: Living the Good Life.* New York, London, Paris: Abbeville Press and Oakland: The Oakland Museum, 1993.

Vaughn, James M., Ann Kantor, Mary Dutton Boehm, Gregg R. Hennessey, Bruce Kamerling, Von-Marie May. "The George White & Anna Gunn Marston House," *The Journal of San Diego History,* Vol. XXXVI, No. 2 and 3, San Diego, California: San Diego Historical Society, Spring/Summer 1990.

Weber, Francis J. *A Bicentennial Compendium of Maynard J. Geiger's The Life And Times of Fray Junipero Serra.* Mission Hills, California, 1984, San Luis Obispo, California: EZ Nature Books, 1988.

White, Samuel G. *The Houses of McKim, Mead & White.* New York: Rizzoli International Publications, Inc., 1998.

White, Samuel G. and Elizabeth White. *McKim, Mead & White: The Masterworks.* New York: Rizzoli International Publications, Inc., 2003.

————. *Stanford White Architect.* New York: Rizzoli International Publications, Inc., 2008.

Winter, Robert. *The California Bungalow.* Los Angeles: Hennessey & Ingalls, Inc., 1980.

————. *Myron Hunt: At Occidental College.* Los Angeles: Occidental College, 1986.

Winter, Robert, ed. *Toward a Simpler Way of Life: The Arts & Crafts Architects of California.* Berkeley, Los Angeles: University of California Press, 1997.

Winter, Robert. *Batchelder Tilemaker.* Los Angeles: Balcony Press, 1999.

Woodbridge, Sally. *Bernard Maybeck: Visionary Architect.* New York, London, Paris: Abbeville Press Publishers, 1992.

Zack, Michele. *Altadena: Between Wilderness and City.* Altadena: Altadena Historical Society, 2004.

Index